Success guides

Leckie ✗ Leckie

Standard Grade
German

Marchia Bennie ✗ Louise Glen

Text copyright © 2007 Marchia Bennie and Louise Glen
Design and layout copyright © 2007 Leckie & Leckie Ltd
Cover image © Phil Talbot / Alamy

1st edition 2007

ISBN 978-1-84372-374-5

Published by
Leckie & Leckie Ltd, 3rd Floor, 4 Queen Street, Edinburgh EH2 1JE

tel: 0131 220 6831   fax: 0131 225 9987

enquiries@leckieandleckie.co.uk   www.leckieandleckie.co.uk

Special thanks to
Clive Bell (content development), Mark Grant (content review), The Partnership Publishing Solutions Ltd.
(design and page make-up), Eduardo Iturralde (illustration), Roda Morrison (copy-editing),
Caleb Rutherford (cover design), Frances Reynolds (proofreading), Fiona Barr (indexing),
Phil Booth (sound engineering), Birte Gross and Ole Schützler (German speakers).

A CIP Catalogue record for this book is available from the British Library.

®Leckie & Leckie is a registered trademark

Leckie & Leckie is a division of Huveaux plc.

Contents

Foreword

Herzlich willkommen!

Welcome to the Leckie & Leckie *Standard Grade German Success Guide*.

This book will take you through key topic areas of Standard Grade German and give you clear explanations of tricky grammar points, as well as vocabulary tips and advice on how to aim for Credit level.

The exercises will help you improve your reading and listening skills and the extended work lets you challenge yourself to raise your standard.

In the guide, you will also find an explanation of how the Standard Grade German exam, Writing Folio and Speaking assessments are structured, and how they fit together to produce your final grade.

Here is a key to features appearing in this guide – they are designed to help you find the best way through the tasks.

'Credit', signify that this material is very difficult, but still highly relevant to the strongest pupils at this level.

This CD icon beside the listening exercises refers to a listening track on the CD, also to the relevant track.

Remember – the key to success is to work steadily through the course: do manageable amounts of work regularly, rather than leaving everything to the last minute.

Goethe once said: 'To be pleased with one's limits is a wretched state.' Bearing this in mind, we wish you all the best with your revision for Standard Grade German.

Remember to aim as high as you can, and give yourself the best possible chance of achieving a good qualification.

Viel Spaß und viel Glück!

Marchia Bennie and Louise Glen

Course summary

Your *Success Guide* deals with the main topics of the Standard Grade German course. It divides them up in this way:

Personal language	Tourist language	Problems
Self	Where I live	Relationships
Family	Transport	Health issues
Hobbies	Holidays	Environment
Education	Eating out	One world

Nearly everything that comes up in your Standard Grade exams in Reading and Listening – and that you do in your Speaking and Writing assessments – can be linked to these topics. They are covered in the first three chapters of this book – Personal Language, Tourist Language and Problems. Topics not falling into these categories (numbers, times and dates) are grouped together for handy reference in the **'Some basic language'** section at the back of the book.

For reference, here is a list of all the topics you need to cover for Standard Grade:

- Personal information given / asked for in polite language
- Members of family, friends and friendship, physical and character description, interpersonal problems and relationships
- Parts of the body, illnesses / accidents
- Making appointments
- Houses / rooms and the ideal house
- Comparison of routine and lifestyles in Scotland and in Germany / other German-speaking countries
- Life in the future; past and future events (in routine)
- Comparison of education system with that of Germany / other German-speaking countries
- Leisure, sports and health issues: healthy eating, exercise, drugs
- TV, film and music
- Other food issues
- Restaurants/menus, making arrangements
- Giving simple and complex directions
- Tourist information, comparison of town/country, helping the environment
- Changing money
- Negotiating transactional problems
- Jobs / working and studying
- Relative merits of jobs
- Work experience
- Future employment
- Travel information
- Travel plans
- Relative merits of different means of transport
- Comparisons between different countries
- Weather
- Future holidays
- Ideal holidays
- Past holidays.

Since having a large vocabulary is a mainstay of achieving success at Standard Grade and beyond, we have put vocabulary into topic areas, in order to make it easier for you to revise.

At the back of the book is a grammar reference section, which will help you to revise some of the most common grammar points you will come across at 'S' Grade. As you become more confident in your use of these, so you should see your efforts in Speaking and Writing improve in particular, although a good grounding in grammar will help you improve your performance in all skill areas.

Alles Gute!

Assessment summary

Assessment at a glance

Standard Grades are all marked according to these grades and levels:

Grades	Levels
1–2	Credit
3–4	General
5–6	Foundation

Reading and Speaking

Reading and Speaking grades are given twice the weight of Listening and Writing (as they are considered the most important by the SQA), and therefore count double when your Overall Grade is made up as an average:

Skills	Weighting
Reading	2
Listening	1
Speaking	2
Writing	1

Here's an example of how this might work in practice:

Skills	Grades	Overall Grade
Reading	3 (so, 3 × 2) → 6	6 + 2 + 4 + 1 = 13 divided by 4 = 3.25
Listening	2	
Speaking	2 (so, 2 × 2) → 4	
Writing	1	

So, the Overall Grade here is grade 3.

Assessment in detail

Reading and Listening Exams

You will sit Reading and Listening exams in German at the same levels; if you are a Credit candidate, you will sit Credit and General papers. If you are a Foundation candidate, you will do the Foundation and General papers.

The Reading and Listening papers are done in May of S4, and your Reading and Listening grades are based solely on how you do on the day of the exam. Many candidates are surprised when they do past paper practice that they are expected to remember some of the vocabulary covered in S1, as well as in S4! You will need to revise **all** of your vocabulary thoroughly, not just from the recent topics!

Reading

Although you are allowed to use a dictionary in the Reading exam, don't start looking up words straight away; follow these hints to help you approach the exam in a calmer way:

- Pace yourself – don't run out of time.
- Read all of the German, including the title.
- Don't assume you will get the correct answer by writing about what is in the picture.
- Read the questions carefully and make sure you know what you are being asked.
- Look at how many marks each question is worth – this will help you to decide how much you should write.
- You won't have time to look up every word in your dictionary. Decide which are the most important words (usually nouns and verbs).

Top Tip
The more words you know, the fewer you will have to look up in the exam. So, make a point of learning vocabulary throughout your course.

Check your answers. After you have written your answers, go back and read over your work. Check that your answers are written in English (unless your answer is a German place name which you cannot translate). Check also that you have not left any gaps. Have a guess if you have to – your guess might be correct.

Use your own dictionary during your Standard Grade course and in the exam, so that you know where to find everything in it.

When using your dictionary:

- you may need to split up compound nouns (two or more nouns joined together), for example, *Bushaltestelle* into *Bus* and *Haltestelle*.
- the word you are looking up may not be in the dictionary in exactly the same form as it appears in the passage. Don't let this put you off! You could be reading a plural form (e.g. *Zeitungen*) or an adjective with an ending (e.g. *natürliches*).
- remember that verbs are entered in your German dictionary in the infinitive form only. In English, when a verb is in the infinitive, it has 'to' in front of it, e.g. 'to go', 'to finish' and 'to do'. In German, when a verb is in the infinitive, it almost always ends in -en, e.g. *gehen* (to go), *beenden* (to finish) and *machen* (to do). So you will find *essen* (to eat) listed in the dictionary, but not *isst* or *gegessen*.

Listening

In the Listening exam, you are *not* allowed a dictionary. The exams are fairly short, each question is introduced in English, you hear each section three times and you can start to write your answers at any time during the playing of the sections.

Hints:

- When listening to each section, don't expect to understand everything – you don't need to!
- Always answer in English.
- Answer the questions concisely. You don't need to write complete sentences.

Speaking

Your final grade for Speaking is taken from the average grade of your three best Speaking assessments, usually done in S4, but some of which you could have done in S3. Speaking assessments are carried out by your German teacher, and sometimes the way they are conducted or graded is checked by the Scottish Qualifications Authority (SQA). Your Speaking assessments will normally be completed by the February or March of your fourth year.

You have to do three different types of Speaking assessment:

- A prepared talk, e.g. *Meine Sommerferien* (max. 2 minutes long; prepared in advance by you; five headings of eight words can be used to help 'kick start' your memory).
- A conversation (max. 5 minutes; usually with your teacher, but can also be with another pupil), e.g. *Meine Freizeit.*
- A role-play (max. 5 minutes; with your teacher or another pupil). This role-play is either *transactional* or *vocational*, so it's about exchanging information or dealing with a particular 'official' situation, e.g. Transactional: *Booking into a hotel*; Vocational: *Working in a tourist information office.*

Bear in mind what examiners are looking for in your Speaking assessments, that is:

- Establishing contact
- Exchanging or presenting information
- Explaining and instructing
- Expressing opinion and reasons
- Expressing understanding.

You need to try to cover these over the three pieces.

Your Speaking assessments are done at the end of a particular topic in German, and you will be given specific instructions by your teacher, along with adequate time and support to prepare. Plenty of practice at home will also be necessary in order to memorise properly.

Writing

The Writing element of your Standard Grade consists of your three best pieces of essay work done under exam conditions in S3 and S4. These are put together as a Folio of your achievements and sent off to the SQA for marking in February or March of your fourth year.

The guideline word counts are as follows:

- Foundation: 25–50 words
- General: 50–100 words
- Credit: 100–200 words.

Remember that it is the overall **quality** of your work, not the quantity, which is the single most important factor in determining the grade.

Examiners are looking for you to be able to present:

- Information
- Opinions
- Reasons

… using a wide variety of vocabulary and structures, as well as showing your ability to use tenses in an appropriate context.

Self 1

Basic vocabulary

General introductions

Hallo!	Hello!
(Guten) Morgen!	(Good) morning!
(Guten) Tag!	Hello! (in the afternoon)
(Guten) Abend!	(Good) evening!
Ich heiße ...	I'm called ...
Mein Name ist ...	My name is ...
Ich bin vierzehn / fünfzehn Jahre alt	I am 14 / 15 years old
Mein Geburtstag ist am einundzwanzigsten November	My birthday is on the 21st November
Ich wohne ...	I live ...
in Schottland	in Scotland
...liegt...	... is (situated) ...
im Norden / in Nordschottland	in the north / north Scotland
im Süden / in Südschottland	in the south / south Scotland
im Westen / in Westschottland	in the west / west Scotland
im Osten / in Ostschottland	in the east / east Scotland

Ich habe ...	I have ...
braune / schwarze / rote / blonde Haare	brown / black / red / blond hair
blaue / braune / grüne Augen	blue / brown / green eyes

Character

Ich bin ...	I am ...
lustig	funny
intelligent	intelligent
faul	lazy
nett	nice
sportlich	sporty

Physical description

Ich bin sehr / ziemlich ...	I'm very / quite ...
groß	tall
klein	small
mittelgroß	average height
dick	fat
schlank	slim

Top Tip
Remember that when you are writing in German, nouns **always** have a capital letter – and not just at the beginning of the sentence, e.g. *Ich habe lange Haare und blaue Augen.*

Extended vocabulary

General information

Ich habe am fünften Juni Geburtstag.	My birthday is on the 5th June.
Ich bin Schotte / Schottin.	I am Scottish.
Ich bin Engländer / Engländerin.	I am English.
Ich komme aus Schottland.	I come from Scotland.
Ich komme aus Polen	I come from Poland.

Physical description

Ich habe ...	I have ...
lange / kurze / schulterlange Haare	long / short / shoulder-length hair
lockige / glatte / wellige Haare	curly / straight / wavy hair
hochstehende / gefärbte Haare	spiky / dyed hair
Ich bin ...	I am ...
stark	strong
schön / hübsch	pretty
gutaussehend	good-looking
Ich trage eine Brille / Kontaktlinsen	I wear glasses / contact lenses

Character

Ich bin ...	I am ...
ziemlich / ganz	quite
ein wenig / ein bisschen	a bit
immer	always
manchmal	sometimes
oft	often
wirklich	really
angenehm	pleasant
zuverlässig	responsible
freundlich	friendly
sympathisch	nice / kind
ruhig	quiet
fleißig	hard-working
doof	silly
launisch	moody
nervig	annoying
ärgerlich	irritating
blöd	silly / stupid
egoistisch	selfish
ungeduldig	impatient

Top Tip
Draw up two columns, headed 'positive Charaktereigenschaften' and 'negative Charaktereigenschaften'; every time you learn another characteristic, you should place it in the correct column.

Quick Test

After learning this vocabulary, cover it up and translate the following sentences into English:

1 Meine Schwester ist manchmal faul, aber immer sympathisch.

2 Ich bin ziemlich klein und habe schulterlange rote Haare.

3 Mein Bruder ist oft nervig und schlecht gelaunt.

4 Ich finde meine Schwester ein bisschen blöd.

5 Ich bin wirklich gutaussehend!

Self 2

Basic grammar

Essential details

Note the different ways of introducing yourself in German:

Ich heiße ...	I'm called ...
Ich bin ...	I am ...
Mein Name ist ...	My name is ...

Trickier details

When you are saying dates, you must remember to add -*en* to the end of the number if it is between 1 and 19, or -*sten* if the number is 20+. Note the ordinal numbers in bold, as these are unusual forms:

Am **ersten** April	on the 1st of April
Am zweiten Januar	on the 2nd of January
Am **dritten** November	on the 3rd of November
Am vierten Juli	on the 4th of July
Am fünften Juni	on the 5th of June
Am sechsten Februar	on the 6th of February
Am **siebten** August	on the 7th of August
Am zehnten Mai	on the 10th of May
Am dreizehnten September	on the 13th of September
Am fünfzehnten März	on the 15th of March
Am neunzehnten Dezember	on the 19th of December
Am zwanzig**sten** Juni	on the 20th of June
Am einundzwanzig**sten** November	on the 21st of November
Am dreißig**sten** Oktober	on the 30th of October
Am einunddreißig**sten** Dezember	on the 31st of December

Note the different ways of asking about others' birthdays / giving your birthday:

Wann hast du Geburtstag?	When is your birthday?
Wann ist dein Geburtstag?	

Ich habe am ... ... Geburtstag.	My birthday is on ... ...
Mein Geburtstag ist am	

Extended grammar

You will need to use a variety of verbs to describe yourself further. Learning the following ones will give you a good basis from which to add some of your own details:

*Ich **heiße** ... / mein Name **ist** ... Rachael.*

*Ich **bin** vierzehn Jahre alt.*

*Ich **wohne** in Glasgow.*

*Ich **bin** Schottin.*

*Ich **bin** groß und schlank.*

*Ich **habe** lange lockige Haare.*

*Ich **habe** blaue Augen.*

*Ich **habe** einen Bruder und zwei Schwestern.*

*Ich **habe** keine Haustiere.*

*Ich **spiele** gern Netzball.*

*Ich **hasse** Computerspiele.*

*Ich **höre** sehr gern Musik.*

*Ich **helfe** nicht gern im Haushalt.*

*Ich **trage** sehr gern meinen Minirock.*

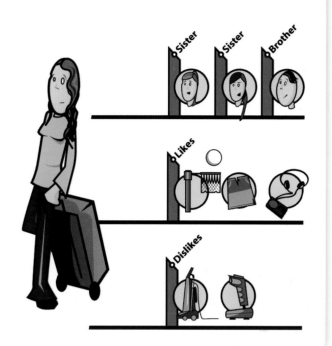

Quick Test

1 Write down the two ways of giving your own birthday in German.

2 Write down the following dates in German:

      on the 8th May

      on the 6th October

      on the 30th November

      on the 12th December

      on the 26th March

3 Now write out a description of yourself. Make it as detailed as you can.

Top Tip

When you are giving dates (e.g. your birthday) you have to remember to give them as ordinal numbers, e.g. the 1st, 2nd, 3rd, etc., in German. When you are **writing** the date, all you have to do is add a full stop after the number: *Montag, den 1. Mai* – Monday, 1st May *Freitag, den 20. Juni* – Friday, 20th June

Self 3

Exercise 1

Now complete this grid in order to test your knowledge and understanding of the 'Self' topic. You will need to use your own class notes, as well as the vocabulary and structures you have learned in this chapter!

German	English
lockige Haare	
grüne Augen	
ziemlich dick	
gutaussehend	
glatte Haare	
launisch	
egoistisch	
vernünftig	
doof	
Ich bin Schottin.	
Ich habe keine Geschwister.	
Ich wohne in Glenrothes.	
Ich bin selten schlecht gelaunt.	
dünn	
Das liegt im Süden.	
	I'm very sporty.
	I've got blue eyes.
	I've got short blond hair.
	I'm quite tall and slim.
	I'm often in a good mood.
	I'm usually friendly.

Top Tip

Remember that if the adjective comes before the noun it is describing, it needs to have an ending; if it comes after the noun, it has no ending, e.g. *Ich habe grüne Augen / meine Augen sind grün.* See pages 105–106 of the Grammar section for more information on adjectives.

Exercise 2

 CREDIT

 1 Read and listen to this description Marko gives of himself and his friends:

- *Also Leute, dann beschreibe ich mich mal für euch … na ja, ich bin relativ gutaussehend, habe braune Augen, blonde Haare, bin ein Meter achtzig groß, wiege fünfundsiebzig Kilo.*
- *Ich bin schlank und sportlich und meistens gut gelaunt!*
- *Ich bin nie aggressiv und habe viele gute Freunde.*
- *Ich bin ziemlich intelligent, aber Mathe finde ich schwierig. Mein Lieblingsfach in der Schule ist Kunst.*
- *In meiner Freizeit höre ich gern Musik und spiele sehr gern am Computer.*
- *Ich habe keine Haustiere, weil ich gegen Tierfell allergisch bin.*
- *Ich mag: Schlafen und Fernsehen.*
- *Mein Freund Hanno ist ein toller Typ – er wohnt ganz in der Nähe, wir kennen uns seit einer Ewigkeit und er ist sehr freundlich. Er ist Einzelkind, aber hat ungefähr zwanzig Fische! Er hat schulterlange schwarze Haare, blaue Augen, ist etwas pummelig und wahnsinnig sympathisch! Er mag: schnelle Autos und Schnee.*
- *Die Ilse ist auch in meiner Clique – sie hat zwei Brüder, die nicht so nett sind, aber trotzdem kommt sie mit ihnen gut zurecht. Sie ist mittelgroß, hat lange glatte Haare, sieht schön aus, ist ein großzügiger Mensch und ist auch stark in Mathe, was sehr gut ist! Sie mag: Katzen und Computerspiele.*

Quick Test

True or false?

1 Marko is quite good looking. ☐

2 He weighs 180 kilos. ☐

3 He finds maths easy to understand. ☐

4 Hanno is an only child. ☐

5 He is slim. ☐

6 He likes rainy days. ☐

7 Ilse gets on well with her brothers. ☐

8 She is pretty. ☐

9 She is good at maths. ☐

10 She likes cats and computer games. ☐

Now look up all the vocabulary from these descriptions which you didn't know previously – and learn it!

Top Tip
In your Listening and Reading exams, you cannot score half a point for any question, so make sure that you give all the **relevant** details!

Family 1

Basic vocabulary

Family – singular

Das ist …	This is …
mein Bruder	my brother
mein Cousin	my (male) cousin
mein Vater	my father
mein Onkel	my uncle
mein Großvater / Opa	my grandfather / grandad
meine Schwester	my sister
meine Kusine	my (female) cousin
meine Mutter	my mother
meine Tante	my aunt
meine Großmutter / Oma	my grandmother / gran

Family – plural

Das sind …	These are …
meine Brüder	my brothers
meine Schwestern	my sisters
meine Eltern	my parents
meine Großeltern	my grandparents

Work

Er / sie geht auf die Schule / Uni.

  he / she goes to school / uni.

Er / sie arbeitet in **einem** …

  he / she works in a / an …

Büro	office
Supermarkt	supermarket
Laden	shop

Krankenhaus	hospital

Er / sie arbeitet in **einer** …

  he / she works in a / an …

Bank	bank
Schule	school
Bibliothek	library
Bäckerei	baker's

Er / sie ist …	he / she is a / an …
Lehrer / Lehrerin	teacher
Arzt / Ärztin	doctor
Zahnarzt / Zahnärztin	dentist
Tierarzt / Tierärztin	vet
Sekretär / Sekretärin	secretary
Elektriker / Elektrikerin	electrician
Mechaniker / Mechanikerin	mechanic
Briefträger / Briefträgerin	postman / woman
Krankenpfleger / Krankenschwester	nurse

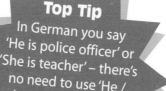

Top Tip

In German you say 'He is police officer' or 'She is teacher' – there's no need to use 'He / she is a …' as we do in English.

Programmierer / *Programmiererin*	programmer
Verkäufer / *Verkäuferin*	shop assistant
Geschäftsmann / *Geschäftsfrau*	businessman / woman
Maurer / Maurerin	bricklayer
Polizist / Polizistin	police officer

Top Tip

In German, you have to make a distinction between male / female job titles; normally, you just add *-in* to the end of the **male** job title; however, there are exceptions! Find them in the list and add in any others you know which don't follow the 'rule'. Make sure you learn them off by heart!

Extended vocabulary

Male members of the family – singular

mein Stiefbruder	my step brother
mein Halbbruder	my half brother
mein älterer Bruder	my older brother
mein jüngerer Bruder	my younger brother
mein Zwillingsbruder	my twin brother
mein Mann	my husband
mein Verlobter	my fiancé
mein Sohn	my son
mein Schwager	my brother-in-law

Male members of the family – plural

meine Stiefbrüder	my step brothers
meine Halbbrüder	my half brothers
meine älteren Brüder	my older brothers
meine jüngeren Brüder	my younger brothers
meine Söhne	my sons

Female members of the family – singular

meine Stiefschwester	my step sister
meine Halbschwester	my half sister
meine ältere Schwester	my older sister
meine jüngere Schwester	my younger sister
meine Zwillingsschwester	my twin sister
meine Frau	my wife
meine Verlobte	my fiancée
meine Tochter	my daughter
meine Schwägerin	my sister-in-law

Female members of the family – plural

meine Stiefschwestern	my step sisters
meine Halbschwestern	my half sisters
meine älteren Schwestern	my older sisters
meine jüngeren Schwestern	my younger sisters
meine Töchter	my daughters

Work

Er / sie besucht …	He / she attends …

(For more information on German schools, see pages 33–35 in the Education topic.)

die Grundschule	primary school
die Gesamtschule	secondary school (comprehensive)
die Uni	university
Er / sie arbeitet bei …	He / she works for …
McDonalds	McDonald's
einer Firma	a company
in einem …	in a …
Schuhgeschäft	shoe shop
Warenhaus	department store
in einer …	in a …
Fabrik	factory
Apotheke	chemist's
Er / sie ist …	He / she is a …
Feuerwehrmann / Feuerwehrfrau	firefighter
Metzger / Metzgerin	butcher
Fabrikarbeiter / Fabrikarbeiterin	factory worker
Student / Studentin	student
Bauer / Bäuerin	farmer
Soldat / Soldatin	soldier
Beamter / Beamtin	civil servant

Exercise 1

Imagine you are introducing your own family and jot down the German you would need.
Start like this:

Das ist … (for singular)

Hier sind …(for plural).

Exercise 2

Test your knowledge of family vocabulary … cover up the lists and note down the following:

My stepsister

My brother-in-law

My male cousin

My fiancée.

Quick Test

Unjumble the following words for jobs and rewrite them correctly:

1 ILOPISITZN

2 HERREL

3 REINÄUB

4 TARZANHZ

5 FRESHFACTÄGUS

Family 2

Basic grammar

You are no doubt aware of the three words for 'a' or 'one' in German – *ein* (masculine), *eine* (feminine) and *ein* (neuter) – and that when you use the various cases in German (see page 93, Grammar section) their endings also have to show changes.

When you are saying 'I have a / one ...' and a member of your family in German, you have to be careful with **masculine nouns** in particular as these have an **ending** on the word *ein* to show that you are using the **accusative case.**

You will remember these phrases from the time when you first learned how to talk about families in German, but here's a quick reminder to jog your memory.

Male family members

*Ich habe **einen** Bruder* .	I have a brother.
*Ich habe **einen** Vater.*	I have a father.
*Ich habe **einen** Stiefvater.*	I have a stepfather.
*Ich habe **einen** Onkel.*	I have an uncle.
*Ich habe **einen** Cousin.*	I have a cousin.
*Ich habe **einen** Halbbruder.*	I have a half brother.
*Ich habe **einen** Großvater.*	I have a grandfather.

Female family members

Ich habe eine Schwester.	I have a sister.
Ich habe eine Mutter.	I have a mother.
Ich habe eine Stiefmutter.	I have a stepmother.
Ich habe eine Tante.	I have an aunt.
Ich habe eine Kusine.	I have a cousin.
Ich habe eine Halbschwester.	I have a half sister.
Ich habe eine Großmutter.	I have a grandmother.

Refer to pages 17–18 for plural forms of family members!

For more information on verb forms, see pages 97–99.

Top Tip
If you are an only child, you can say either *'Ich bin Einzelkind'* or *'Ich habe keine Geschwister'.* Everyone can use the *'**kein / e / en**'* construction to talk about a member of the family they **don't** have, e.g. *Ich habe keine Cousins / Ich habe keinen Großvater.*

Extended grammar

No / Not a

The way to say 'I don't have ... e.g. brothers / sisters' is easy in German; you use the appropriate form of the word 'kein' which follows the 'ein / eine / ein' pattern:

Ich habe **keine** Geschwister.   I have no brothers or sisters.

Sie hat **keinen** Bruder.   She doesn't have a brother.

Wir haben **keinen** Großvater.   We don't have a grandfather.

Er hat **keine** Tante.   He hasn't got an aunt.

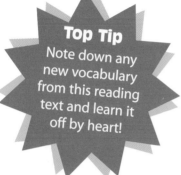

Top Tip
Note down any new vocabulary from this reading text and learn it off by heart!

Read the information given by Uwe and answer the questions that follow:

Hallo! Mein Name ist Uwe. Ich bin fünfzehn Jahre alt und wohne in Hannover in Norddeutschland. Ich habe einen Bruder, Stefan und eine Schwester, Julia. Stefan ist einundzwanzig Jahre alt und wohnt in Hameln. Er ist Student und er spielt gern Fußball. Julia ist zwölf und geht aufs Gymnasium. Sie fährt gern mit dem Rad. Meine Eltern heißen Brigitte und Johann. Meine Mutter ist Bibliothekerin und mein Vater ist Ingenieur. Ich habe zwei Großmütter und einen Großvater, vier Onkeln und drei Tanten. Ich habe drei Kusinen und vier Cousins, sie sind alle jünger als ich! Ich bin groß und hübsch! In meiner Freizeit spiele ich Gitarre und ich gehe regelmäßig schwimmen. Ich besuche das Gymnasium und bekomme eine Menge Hausaufgaben, was sehr nervig ist!

CREDIT

1 Where exactly is his hometown situated?
2 Give three pieces of information about Uwe's brother.
3 What jobs do his parents have?
4 What does he say about his cousins?
5 What does he think of homework?

Quick Test

Match up the family members below

1 Brüder	a) male cousin
2 Schwester	b) gran
3 Kusine	c) brothers and sisters
4 Väter	d) sister
5 Schwestern	e) female cousin
6 Cousin	f) fathers
7 Vater	g) brother
8 Geschwister	h) sisters
9 Oma	i) brothers
10 Bruder	j) father

Family 3

Exercise 1

Test yourself on the family vocabulary covered in this unit:

German	English	Male jobs	Female jobs
Schwägerin		Pilot	
Töchter			Bäuerin
Vetter		Zahnarzt	
Verlobte		Lehrer	
Opa			Krankenschwester
Geschwister			
Zwillingsbruder			
Stiefschwester			
Söhne			
Halbschwester			

Top Tip

Make sure you know which towns and cities change their spelling when translated into German; some of the most common are *München* (Munich), *Wien* (Vienna), *Köln* (Cologne), *Hannover* (Hanover), *Nürnberg* (Nuremberg) and *Hameln* (Hamelin) – make a note of any others you come across!

Exercise 2

Read this text and listen to the description of Helmut's family. Note the information required in the grid which follows:

Also, jetzt stelle ich euch meine Familie vor: mein Großvater, Hans. Er wurde in München geboren. Er ist einundneunzig Jahre alt, klein und ein bisschen dick mit einem weißen Vollbart und er ist ein sehr geduldiger und freundlicher Mensch. Er war Polizist von Beruf.

CREDIT

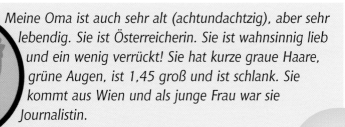

Meine Oma ist auch sehr alt (achtundachtzig), aber sehr lebendig. Sie ist Österreicherin. Sie ist wahnsinnig lieb und ein wenig verrückt! Sie hat kurze graue Haare, grüne Augen, ist 1,45 groß und ist schlank. Sie kommt aus Wien und als junge Frau war sie Journalistin.

CREDIT

CREDIT

Das ist mein Vater, Thomas. Er ist fünfzig Jahre alt und arbeitet als Geschäftsmann für eine große Firma in Linz in Österreich. Er ist freundlich und ziemlich locker mit uns Kindern, was uns sehr freut! Er ist mittelgroß und hat kurze, lockige Haare und trägt eine Brille.

… und das ist meine Mutter, Sophia. Sie ist Schweizerin und ist sechsundvierzig Jahre alt. Meine Mutter ist hübsch und klein und sie hat schulterlange schwarze Haare und braune Augen. Sie ist Opernsängerin und arbeitet überall in der Welt, aber nur sechs Monate pro Jahr. Wenn sie zu Hause ist, ist sie manchmal launisch, weil sie so müde ist, aber sie kann wirklich sehr lieb sein. Sie ist immer streng!

CREDIT

Family member	Age	Physical description	Character	Job	Any other details

Quick Test

Which member of the family …

- is Swiss?
- is quite fat?
- wears glasses?
- is sometimes moody?
- was a police officer?
- is a bit mad?

Top Tip
Pick out any new vocabulary from the descriptions above and put it into lists of physical descriptions and characteristics – then learn it by heart!

Hobbies 1

Basic vocabulary

Places you go to

(See pages 92–93 of the Grammar section for notes on cases.)

Ich gehe …	I go …
in den Jugendklub	to the youth club
in den Park	to the park
in die Stadt	to the / into town
in die Disko	to the disco
ins Fußballstadion	to the football stadium
ins Sportzentrum	to the sports centre
ins Hallenbad	to the pool
ins Kino	to the cinema
ins Einkaufszentrum	to the shopping centre
ins Theater	to the theatre
ins Eisstadion	to the ice rink
auf Partys	to parties

Sports

Ich spiele gern …	I like to play …
Fußball	football
Rugby	rugby
Kricket	cricket
Handball	handball
Tischtennis	table tennis
Hockey	hockey

Ich gehe gern …	I like to go …
joggen	jogging
wandern	walking
windsurfen	wind-surfing
Schlittschuh laufen	ice-skating

Ich schwimme gern.	I like swimming.
Ich reite gern.	I like riding.
Ich fahre gern Rad.	I like cycling.

Music

Ich spiele …	I play …
Klavier	the piano
Geige	the violin
Klarinette	the clarinet
Flöte	the flute
Blockflöte	the recorder
Schlagzeug	the drums

Reading

Ich lese gern …	I like reading …
Zeitschriften	magazines
Zeitungen	newspapers
Romane	novels

TV and films

Ich sehe gern …	I like watching …
fern	TV
Krimis	detective programmes
Sportsendungen	sports programmes
Seifenopern	soap operas
Serien	series
Musiksendungen	music
Dokumentare	documentaries
Liebesfilme	romantic films
Abenteuerfilme	adventure films
Komödien	comedies
Schauspiele	plays

Top Tip
Have you noticed that you don't say 'I play **the** flute' in German? It's as if you say 'I play flute'.

Extended vocabulary 1

Hobbies

How to say what you like doing best using **regular** word order:

Ich ... am liebsten ...   I like to do ... the best.
Ich spiele am liebsten Fußball.
       I like playing football the best.
Ich höre am liebsten Musik.
       I like listening to music the best.
Ich sehe am liebsten fern.
       I like watching TV the best.
Ich tanze am liebsten.   I like dancing the best.
Ich singe am liebsten.   I like singing the best.
Ich gehe am liebsten einkaufen.
       I like shopping the best.

How to say what you like doing best using **inverted** word order:

*Am liebsten **spiele ich** Hockey.*
       I like playing hockey the best.
*Am liebsten **koche ich.***   I like cooking the best.
*Am liebsten **fahre ich** mit dem Rad.*
       I like cycling the best.
*Am liebsten **bastele ich.***
       I like doing crafts the best.
*Am liebsten **reite ich.***
       I like horse riding the best.
*Am liebsten **lese ich.***   I like reading the best.

You can vary the word order in the same way to talk about free time / after school activities:

Ich spiele Gitarre in meiner Freizeit.
       I play the guitar in my free time.
Ich gehe in meiner Freizeit spazieren.
       I go for walks in my spare time.
Ich spiele Schach nach der Schule.
       I play chess after school.
Ich treffe meine Freunde nach der Schule.
       I meet my friends after school.
*In meiner Freizeit **spiele ich** in einer Band.*
       In my spare time I play in a band.
*In meiner Freizeit **gehe ich** schwimmen.*
       In my free time I go swimming.

*Nach der Schule **spiele ich** Karten.*
       After school I play cards.
*Nach der Schule **koche ich** das Abendessen.*
       After school I cook dinner.

Another way of talking about hobbies is to use the following construction:

Mein Lieblingshobby ist Schwimmen.
       My favourite hobby is swimming.
Mein Lieblingshobby ist Skifahren.
       My favourite hobby is ski-ing.

When you want to say something negative about hobbies and such like, you can use the simple construction **nicht gern**:

*Ich gehe **nicht gern** angeln.*
       I don't like fishing.
*Ich höre **nicht gern** Rockmusik.*
       I don't like listening to rock music.

Or even stronger:

*Ich **kann** Computerspiele **nicht leiden.***
       I can't stand computer games.
*Ich **hasse** Hausaufgaben.*
       I hate homework.

TV and films

Spionagefilme	spy films
Kinderfilme	children's films
Sci-Fi Filme	science-fiction films
Kriegsfilme	war films
Actionfilme	action films
die Nachrichten	the news
die Werbung	adverts
der Wetterbericht	the weather forecast

Top Tip

There are several different ways of saying what you like doing in your spare time. You should vary the word order you use to make your Speaking assessment or Folio piece sound more interesting, more like fluent German and less like a list!

Quick Test CREDIT

Read this paragraph and answer the questions below:

In meiner Freizeit mache ich allerlei Sachen; jeden Tag nach der Schule übe ich eine Stunde Klavier, danach mache ich meine Hausaufgaben und dann sehe ich fern – am liebsten sehe ich Musiksendungen und Talkshows. Ich hasse Dokumentarfilme und Natursendungen! Ich lese am liebsten im Bett, meistens Krimis. Am Wochenende treffe ich mich mit meinen Freunden; oft gehen wir ins Einkaufszentrum, wenn wir Geld haben und manchmal gehen wir auf eine Party. In den Sommerferien gehe ich schwimmen oder wandern.

- Mention three things she does after school.
- What doesn't she like on TV?
- What does she do at weekends?
- How do you know she likes music?
- When does she go swimming or walking?

Hobbies 2

Basic grammar

Regular and irregular verbs

If you look back at some of the sentences you have used so far in this section, you will notice that there are certain patterns to the verb endings you have used:

Ich **gehe** oft ins Kino.	I often go to the cinema.
Ich **höre** gern Musik.	I like listening to music.
Ich **koche** gern.	I like cooking.
Ich **spiele** Tennis.	I play tennis.

In German, verbs are either regular or irregular. Regular verbs follow certain patterns. The four verbs shown above are regular and the *ich* form ends in -*e*. Look at how to form regular verbs from the table below.

Verbs are 'doing' or 'being' words, for example, 'go', 'work', 'have' and 'is'. They are very important: without a verb you have no sentence!

The Present Tense (see pages 97–98 of the Grammar section)

All verbs have tenses. Tenses tell you when things occur:

• the **Present Tense** is used to describe what **is happening** or what **happens** on a regular basis.

To form the Present Tense with **regular verbs**, remove -*en* from the infinitive and add the endings in bold:

gehen		**to go**	**Extra info**
ich	geh**e**	I go (I am going)	
du	geh**st**	you go (you are going)	*du* = young person or an adult you know very well, e.g. a relative
er	geh**t**	he goes (he is going)	
sie	geh**t**	she goes (she is going)	
es	geh**t**	it goes (it is going)	
man	geh**t**	one goes (one is going)	*man* = 'you' in general
wir	geh**en**	we go (we are going)	
ihr	geh**t**	you go (you are going)	*ihr* = the plural of du
Sie	geh**en**	you go (you are going)	*Sie* = the polite form for you, singular and plural
sie	geh**en**	they go (they are going)	

Some verbs are **irregular.** They change in the **du** and **er / sie / es** forms, and often have a vowel shift from the infinitive form, e.g. **sehen** – to see.

ich sehe	I see
du siehst	you see
er sieht	he sees
sie sieht	she sees
es sieht	it sees
man sieht	one sees
wir sehen	we see
ihr seht	you see
Sie sehen	you see
sie sehen	they see

Top Tip
Now that you have copied down these **VIV**s (**V**ery **I**mportant **V**erbs), you should stick them onto your bedroom wall and recite them every day until you can do it with your eyes closed!

sein (to be) and **haben** (to have) are very important verbs – copy them down now on a sheet of paper and learn them off by heart!

sein	**to be**	**haben**	**to have**
ich bin	I am	*ich habe*	I have
du bist	you are	*du hast*	you have
er ist	he is	*er hat*	he has
sie ist	she is	*sie hat*	she has
es ist	it is	*es hat*	it has
man ist	one is	*man hat*	one has
wir sind	we are	*wir haben*	we have
ihr seid	you are	*ihr habt*	you have
Sie sind	you are	*Sie haben*	you have
sie sind	they are	*sie haben*	they have

learning off by heart

Extended grammar

Using inverted word order

As mentioned earlier in this chapter (see page 25), you need to ensure that you use a variety of constructions when completing a Speaking or Writing assessment to make sure that you do not simply reel off lists of hobbies. This could be a bit boring! You need to liven up what you are saying or writing with a few time phrases. You have to be careful if you use a time phrase to start the sentence, as you have to use inverted word order. However, if you do this accurately in both your Speaking and Writing assessments, it will certainly count in your favour!

Ich gehe oft ins Kino.	I often go to the cinema.
*Oft **gehe ich** ins Kino.*	I often go to the cinema.

See pages 107–108 of the Grammar section for more information on word order.

Time phrases

Add these to your sentences to make your speaking and writing more interesting … and remember to take care with the word order!

Find the English translations for these time phrases:

- *normalerweise*
- *im Großen und Ganzen*
- *jeden Tag*
- *am Wochenende*
- *in den Ferien*
- *samstags*
- *nach der Schule*
- *am Nachmittag*
- *im Sommer*
- *einmal pro Woche*
- *jeden Morgen*
- *manchmal*

Top Tip
Get used to using inverted word order by practising both forms of sentences where possible; e.g. *Ich gehe manchmal schwimmen = Manchmal gehe ich schwimmen; Mein Bruder hört am liebsten Rockmusik = Am liebsten hört mein Bruder Rockmusik.*

Quick Test

Now try putting the following time phrases into German:

- On Fridays
- Every month
- Twice a week
- In the winter
- Generally

Hobbies 3

Exercise 1

Read this account of Brigitte's free time activities. Fill in the gaps with the correct form of the verbs given in brackets.

Am Wochenende **schlafe** (schlafen) ich mich gut aus, weil ich von der Schule so müde _____ (sein). Zuerst _____ (gehen) ich in die Stadt, wo ich meine Freunde (treffen). Wir _____ (gehen) in den Park, um Fußball zu spielen. Unsere Mannschaft kann echt gut kicken! Danach _____ (gehen) wir ins Café, um uns zu erholen. Ich _____ (sein) Mitglied eines Jugendzentrums und dort _____ (spielen) ich Tischtennis oder Schach. Manchmal aber _____ (faulenzen) ich nur und _____ (sehen) fern oder ich _____ (lesen) eine Zeitschrift. Meine Schwester Julia _____ (spielen) gern mit dem Computer, _____ (sehen) gern fern und _____ (fahren) auch gern mit dem Rad.

Exercise 2

Listen to this account of Uli's weekend. Read the sentences below and choose which of the two statements is the correct one.

1 *Ich lese ziemlich viel – **meistens** Zeitungen / Zeitschriften.*
2 ***Ab und zu** gehe ich ins Jugendzentrum / Einkaufszentrum.*
3 ***Manchmal** sehe ich fern / einen Film an.*
4 *Meine Freunde und ich gehen **oft** schwimmen / eislaufen.*
5 ***Im Sommer** faulenze ich / koche ich.*

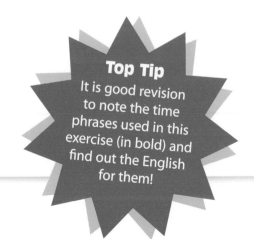

Top Tip
It is good revision to note the time phrases used in this exercise (in bold) and find out the English for them!

Extended vocabulary 2 · CREDIT

Other activities

zeichnen	to draw	*simsen*	to text
malen	to paint	*stricken*	to knit
ausgehen	to go out	*nähen*	to sew
Freunde besuchen	to visit friends	*Sport treiben*	to do sport
Karate / Judo machen	to do karate / judo	*Briefmarken sammeln*	to collect stamps

Exercise 3 · 4 ⊖

Read through and listen to this questionnaire from a German magazine and choose the answer best suited to you and your interests: see what your answers say about you at the end!

1 *Treiben Sie Sport:*   a. *oft?*—b. *manchmal?*—c. *nie?*
2 *Spielen Sie:*   a. *Tennis?*—b. *Fußball?*—c. *mit dem Computer?*
3 *Gehen Sie:*   a. *schwimmen?*—b. *spazieren?*—c. *einkaufen?*
4 *Sehen Sie gern:*   a. *Fußballspiele?*—b. *Rugbyspiele?*—c. *fern?*
5 *Lesen Sie gern:*   a. *Krimis?*—b. *Liebesgeschichten?*—c. *im Bett?*
6 *Essen Sie meistens:*   a. *gesund?*—b. *vegetarisch?*—c. *Schokolade?*

Resultaten

Meistens a. – Sie sind superfit!

Meistens b. – Sie sind sehr fit!

Meistens c. – Sie sind … ähm … nicht so fit!

Quick Test

Now use your answers to help you write a paragraph about yourself in German, mentioning your hobbies and interests. Be careful when changing the verb forms to *ich* and watch out for the word order – you could start off your paragraph like this:

Ich bin ziemlich sportlich; ich spiele regelmäßig Badminton und Tischtennis im Jugendklub. Zweimal pro Woche … ich …

Top Tip
Notice that the formal German word for 'you' – *Sie* – is used in this survey. In the Present Tense with regular verbs, the ending is usually *-en*.

Education 1

Basic vocabulary

Subjects

In der Schule lerne ich …	At school I have / take …
Englisch	English
Deutsch	German
Französisch	French
Spanisch	Spanish
Italienisch	Italian
Latein	Latin
Fremdsprachen	modern / foreign languages
Mathe / Mathematik	maths / mathematics
Informatik	IT
Biologie	biology
Chemie	chemistry

Physik	physics
Naturwissenschaften	science
Geschichte	history
Politik / Gemeinschaftskunde	politics / modern studies
Erdkunde / Geographie	geography
Religion	RME
Wirtschaftslehre	business studies
Kunst	art
Musik	music
Sport	PE
Hauswirtschaft	HE
Sozialkunde	PSE
Technisches Zeichnen / Technik	CDT

Likes and dislikes

Mein Lieblingsfach ist …	My favourite subject is …
Meine Lieblingsfächer sind …	My favourite subjects are …
Deutsch gefällt mir.	I like German.
Wirtschaftslehre gefällt mir nicht.	I don't like business studies.
Chemie gefällt mir gar nicht.	I don't like chemistry at all.
Französisch und Englisch gefallen mir sehr.	I really like French and English.
Sport und Musik gefallen mir nicht.	I don't like PE or music.

Top Tip
Remember to learn vocabulary in small, manageable chunks! Try to learn the names of subjects which are logically grouped together, such as the names for all the different foreign languages, then move on to the sciences, etc.

Extended vocabulary

CREDIT

Describing schools

Ich gehe auf … / Ich besuche …	I go to … / I attend …
Er / sie geht auf … / besucht …	He / she goes to … / attends …
eine Grundschule	a primary school
eine Gesamtschule	a comprehensive school
eine Privatschule	a private school
eine Privatschule für Mädchen / Jungen	a private school for girls / boys

Es gibt ungefähr tausend Schüler und siebzig Lehrer.

There are approximately 1000 pupils and 70 teachers.

Die Schule befindet sich in der Stadtmitte / am Stadtrand.

The school is situated in the town centre / on the outskirts of town.

etwa 5 Kilometer von der Stadt entfernt	about 5 kms from town
auf dem Land	in the country

Top Tip

In German, the school building is often referred to as '*das Haus*' which is where the job title '*der Hausmeister*' comes from – look up this word (if you don't already know it) to discover the most important job in the school!

Opinions about your school

für + pro

Es gibt eine gute Atmosphäre.

There's a good atmosphere.

Die Schüler und die Lehrer kommen miteinander gut aus.

The pupils and staff get on well.

Das Gebäude ist in gutem Zustand.

The building is in a good condition.

Die Sportanlagen sind gut.

The sports facilities are good.

Die Schule ist gut ausgerüstet.

The school is well equipped.

Wir haben viele Arbeitsgemeinschaften (AG's).

There are lots of extra-curricular clubs.

gegen – contra

Es gibt einen Mangel an Disziplin.

There's a lack of discipline.

Es gibt wenig Respekt zwischen Lehrern und Schülern.

There's little respect between pupils and staff.

Einige Schüler benehmen sich schlecht.

Some pupils are badly behaved.

Einige Schüler sind unmotiviert.

Some pupils are unmotivated.

Es gibt zu viele Klassenarbeiten.

There are too many assessments.

Facilities / Equipment

Wir haben ...	We have ...
Es gibt ... (remember to use the accusative case)	There is / are ...
einen Schulhof	a playground
einen Sportplatz	a sports ground
einen Computerraum	an IT suite
eine Bibliothek	a library
eine Turnhalle	a sports hall
eine Aula	an assembly hall
eine Kantine	a canteen
ein Schwimmbad	a pool
ein Labor	a laboratory
ein Café	a café
ein Lehrerzimmer	a staffroom
Tennisplätze	tennis courts

School rules

Die Hausordnung	School rules
Man muss eine Uniform tragen.	You have to wear a uniform.
Man darf nicht im Klassenzimmer essen.	You're not allowed to eat in class.
Man muss rechtzeitig zur Schule kommen.	You have to get to school on time.
Man darf nicht im Gang rennen.	You're not allowed to run in the corridors.
Man darf nicht rauchen.	You're not allowed to smoke.
Man darf nicht frech sein.	You're not allowed to be cheeky.

Quick Test

Translate the following statements about school into English:

1 *Chemie ist mein Lieblingsfach.*

2 *Kunst gefällt mir gar nicht.*

3 *Ich besuche eine Gesamtschule.*

4 *In der Schule muss man eine Uniform tragen.*

5 *Man darf nicht im Gang skaten.*

Now rewrite these statements, changing the information to suit you and your school.

Quick Test

Imagine what your ideal school would be like and write a description of it in German using the vocabulary from this chapter. Alternatively, you could write a description of a nightmare school ...!

Start off with a few simple details like this ...

Meine Schule heißt ... Das ist eine Gesamt schule in der Stadtmitte von ... und hat ungefähr fünfhundert Schüler und sechzig Lehrer. In der Schule muss man eine Uniform tragen, man darf nicht im Gang rennen und man muss nicht zu spät zur Schule kommen. Ich finde die Hausordnung einfach blöd, weil ...

Education 2

Basic grammar

Daily routine at school

Ich stehe um halb sieben auf.	I get up at 6.30.
Ich wasche mich.	I get washed.
Ich dusche.	I have a shower.
Ich ziehe mich an.	I get dressed.
Ich frühstücke.	I have breakfast.
Ich gehe um acht Uhr dreißig aus dem Haus.	I leave the house at 8.30.
Ich bin um Viertel vor neun in der Schule.	I get to school at 8.45.
Der Unterricht fängt um neun Uhr an.	Lessons start at 9.
Eine Stunde dauert fünfzig Minuten.	A period lasts 50 minutes.
Die Pause ist um zehn Uhr zwanzig.	Break is at 10.20.
Die Mittagspause ist um Viertel vor eins.	Lunch is at 12.45.
Normalerweise esse ich in der Kantine.	I usually eat in the canteen.
Die Schule ist um halb vier aus.	School finishes at 3.30.
Ich bin um vier Uhr zu Hause.	I get home at 4.
Zuerst mache ich meine Hausaufgaben	I do my homework first
… und danach esse ich zu Abend.	… then I have my evening meal.
Ich sehe eine Stunde fern	I watch TV for an hour
… dann gehe ich ins Bett.	… then I go to bed.

Reflexive verbs

Reflexive verbs often convey an action you do to yourself, e.g. wash, shower, get dressed, get changed, etc.

Reflexive verbs have an extra word after the actual subject pronoun which means 'to myself' or 'to themselves' – in other words, the action reflects back on the subject pronoun. There are two forms of reflexive verbs in German; most are used with accusative (direct) reflexive pronouns, and some reflexive verbs use the dative (indirect) reflexive pronouns instead. See page 104 of the Grammar section for more examples.

You will find a lot of these verbs in the Daily Routine topic (the reflexive pronouns are shown in bold below).

Ich wasche mich.	I get washed.
Ich ziehe mich an.	I get dressed.

Obviously, the reflexive pronoun changes according to the subject pronoun:

ich wasche mich	I get washed	du wäschst dich	you get washed
er / sie / es / man wäscht sich	he / she / it / one gets washed		
wir waschen uns	we get washed	ihr wascht euch	you get washed
Sie / sie waschen sich	you / they get washed		

Extended grammar

CREDIT

You do not have to use the Future Tense all the time!
Look at these expressions below:

Nächstes Jahr mache ich 'Higher' Englisch. Next year I'm taking 'Higher' English.

Nächstes Jahr möchte ich 'Higher' Deutsch machen. Next year I'd like to take 'Higher' German.

Nächstes Jahr hoffe ich, 'Higher' Französisch zu machen. Next year I hope to take 'Higher' French.

Nächstes Jahr will ich 'Higher' Mathe machen. Next year I want to take 'Higher' maths.

Nächstes Jahr werde ich 'Higher' Kunst machen. Next year I will take 'Higher' art.

Ich möchte mit 16 die Schule verlassen. I'd like to leave school at 16.

Ich hoffe, auf die Uni zu gehen. I hope to go to university.

Ich will weiterstudieren. I want to continue studying.

To give reasons for your current / future choices, you will need to use conjunctions such as *weil*, or *da*; your teacher will probably have gone over the grammar rules associated with such conjunctions. However, if you need to refresh your memory, refer to page 108 of the Grammar section.

Top Tip
When you are writing a Folio piece, it is important that you use a wide variety of tenses and expressions. Use some of the following phrases to make your essay flow better and look less like a list!

Quick Test

Match up these phrases to help you describe your daily routine in German.

1	*Um halb acht*	**a)**	*ist die Schule aus.*
2	*Nach der Schule*	**b)**	*frühstücke ich.*
3	*Um neun Uhr*	**c)**	*gehe ich ins Bett.*
4	*Um halb vier*	**d)**	*mache ich meine Hausaufgaben.*
5	*Am Nachmittag*	**e)**	*fängt der Unterricht an.*
6	*Um zehn Uhr*	**f)**	*sehe ich fern.*

Education 3

Exercise 1

CREDIT

Susanne is writing about her school and her daily routine. Answer the questions which follow in English. The number in brackets indicates how many points of information you need to give.

Hallo, mein Name ist Susanne und ich besuche die Ricarda-Huch-Schule in Hannover. Meine Schule ist ein Gymnasium und befindet sich am Stadtrand. Ich bin im zehnten Jahrgang. Ich lerne Deutsch, Englisch, Französisch, Latein, Mathe, Chemie und Reli. Ich habe keine Lieblingsfächer, aber Latein gefällt mir gut, obwohl es manchmal schwierig und kompliziert sein kann. Chemie kann ich nicht leiden, ich finde es bloß stinklangweilig und habe kein gutes Verhältnis zu meinem Lehrer; er hört einfach nicht zu! Ich komme mit den anderen Lehrern ziemlich gut aus, aber wir bekommen eine Menge Hausaufgaben, was nicht so toll ist! Morgens stehe ich um sechs Uhr auf und ich gehe um sieben aus dem Haus. Ich fahre mit der Bahn zur Schule. Die erste Stunde beginnt um Viertel vor acht. Um fünf nach zehn haben wir eine Pause. In der Pause trinke ich eine Cola, und ich plaudere mit meinen Freunden. Dann gibt es noch zwei Stunden, und danach bin ich normalerweise frei, aber meistens habe ich eine AG in Sport. Ich gehe gegen drei Uhr nach Hause, mache meine Hausaufgaben, sehe eine Stunde fern, spreche mit Freunden am Telefon, surfe am Computer, esse zu Abend, lese eine Zeitschrift und gehe gegen halb elf ins Bett. Unter der Woche bin ich oft müde!

1	Where is her school situated?	(1)
2	What comments does she make about Latin?	(2)
3	What does she say about her chemistry teacher?	(2)
4	How does she get to school?	(1)
5	What does she do at break?	(2)
6	Give any five details about her after school routine.	(5)

Top Tip

When you are doing reading comprehension questions, both for practice and in exam situations, get into the habit of always looking at the rubric (the line(s) above the text which set the scene) as these can help you establish what kind of vocabulary may be used; then look at the questions themselves, in order to see exactly where you need to focus your attention – you will notice that you don't have to know every word in the text to be able to get the meaning, and it saves you from grabbing at the dictionary and wasting valuable time!

Quick Test

Now look back over the text and find the English for the following – remember to make a note of both the German and the English vocab!

1 I attend
2 I like Latin
3 just ultra boring
4 lots of
5 normally
6 after that (one word)

Exercise 2

Listen to these pupils talking about their school and answer the questions which follow – the number in brackets indicates how many points of information you need to give:

Ich heiße Bernd. Ich habe drei Stunden Sportunterricht pro Woche; Sport macht Spaß, besonders wenn wir Badminton spielen, aber es kann oft anstrengend sein. Ich hasse Geschichte!

Ich heiße Julia. Ich lerne am liebsten Französisch und Latein, obwohl es manchmal kompliziert ist. Geschichte gefällt mir nicht!

Ich heiße Klaus. Englisch gefällt mir nicht; der Lehrer ist zu locker und spricht fast die ganze Zeit Deutsch und wir lernen nichts. Geschichte, das kann ich nicht leiden! Stinklangweilig!

Ich bin Jenny. Für mich sind Mathe und Informatik die wichtigsten Fächer; man lernt mit den Computern umzugehen und ich hoffe in der Zukunft als Programmiererin zu arbeiten. Geschichte ist langweilig!

1 How many periods of PE does Bernd have? (1)
2 What other comments does he make about it? (2)
3 Which languages does Julia study and what does she say about them? (3)
4 What is Jenny's opinion of maths and IT? (1)
5 What type of job would she like to do in the future? (1)
6 Why doesn't Klaus enjoy English? (2)
7 They all dislike one subject in particular – which one is it? (1)

Now look at the text and find four different ways to say you don't like a subject and ... learn them off by heart!

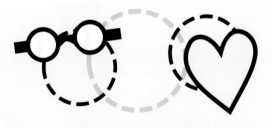

learning off by heart

Top Tip
Cover up the text before you embark on this, and listen to each section three times, to make the exercise more like exam practice.

Where I live 1

Basic vocabulary

Area

Ich wohne ...	I live ...
Wir wohnen ...	We live ...
in einem Doppelhaus	in a semi-detached
in einem Einfamilienhaus	in a detached house
in einem Reihenhaus	in a terraced house
in der Stadtmitte	in the town centre
am Stadtrand	on the outskirts
in einer Wohnsiedlung	in a housing estate
auf dem Lande	in the country
in der Nähe von ...	near ...
nicht weit von ...	not far from ..
fünf Kilometer von ... entfernt	five kilometres away from
( ) ist eine ...	( ) is a ...
historische	historic
kleine	small
schöne	beautiful
Stadt	town
( ) ist eine Industriestadt	( ) is an industrial town
( ) ist eine Touristenstadt mit vierzigtausend Einwohnern	( ) is a tourist town with 40,000 inhabitants
in Nordschottland	in the north of Scotland
in Südschottland	in the south of Scotland
in Westschottland	in the west of Scotland
in Ostschottland	in the east of Scotland
in Mittelschottland	in central Scotland

Floors and rooms

Im Keller gibt es ...	in the basement there is ...
eine Garage	a garage
einen Hobbyraum	a hobby room
eine Waschküche	a utility room
Im Erdgeschoss haben wir...	on the ground floor we have ...
ein Arbeitszimmer	a study
ein Esszimmer	a dining room
eine Küche	a kitchen
einen Flur	a hall
eine Toilette	a toilet
ein Wohnzimmer	a living room
im ersten Stock gibt es ...	on the 1st floor there is ...
das Elternschlafzimmer	mum and dad's room
das Gästezimmer	the spare room
mein Schlafzimmer	my room
im zweiten Stock haben wir ...	on the second floor we have ...
den Dachboden	the attic

Bedroom

Mein Schlafzimmer ist ...	My bedroom is ...
ziemlich / sehr ...	quite / very ...
klein / groß	small / big
schön	lovely
Es gibt ...	There is ...
ein Bett	a bed
einen Computer	a computer
einen CD Spieler	a CD player

Nordschottland

Westschottland **Mittelschottland** **Ostschottland**

Südschottland

Top Tip
Notice that to say in a place that's feminine (*die* words), you say 'in einer ...' To say in a place that's masculine or neuter (*der, das* words), you say 'in einem ...' See the Grammar section, pages 92–93, for cases.

einen Kleiderschrank	a wardrobe
einen Teppich	a carpet
ein Bücherregal	a bookshelf
eine Lampe	a light
eine Uhr	a clock
einige CDs	some CDs
einige Posters von ...	some posters of ...
meine Schulsachen	my school things
Dort / da ...	there ...
mache ich meine Hausaufgaben	I do my homework
höre ich Musik	I listen to music
spiele ich auf dem Computer	I play on the computer

eine Bibliothek	a library
eine Brücke	a bridge
eine Disko	a disco
eine Polizeiwache	a police station
eine Post	a post office
eine (Reifen)fabrik	a (tyre) factory
eine Tankstelle	a filling station
viele Betriebe	lots of businesses
einige Cafés	some cafés
ein paar Denkmäler	a few monuments
einige Gasthäuser	some pubs
viele Geschäfte	lots of shops
einige Hotels	some hotels
ein paar Kaufhäuser	a few department stores
viele Restaurants	lots of restaurants
viele Wohnblöcke	lots of blocks of flats

Town places

In meiner Stadt gibt es ...	In my town there is ...
ein Einkaufszentrum	a shopping centre
ein Jugendzentrum	a youth centre
ein Kino	a cinema
ein Krankenhaus	a hospital
ein Museum	a museum
ein Rathaus	a town hall
ein Schloss	a castle
ein Sportzentrum	a sports centre
ein Stadion	a stadium
ein Theater	a theatre
ein Verkehrsamt	a tourist office
einen Bahnhof	a station
einen Busbahnhof	a bus station
einen Dom	a cathedral
einen Fußballplatz	a football pitch
einen Markt	a market
einen Marktplatz	a market square
einen Nachtklub	a night-club
einen Park	a park
einen Supermarkt	a supermarket
eine Bank	a bank

Quick Test

Now let's try a brainteaser! Write down on a sheet of paper the word

NORDWESTDEUTSCHLAND

Now find a word that begins with each of these letters from these two pages and write each one vertically under each letter, e.g.

NORDWESTDEUTSCHLAND

a

c

h

t

k

l

u

b

Where I live 2

Basic grammar

These phrases can be used to start talking about where you live:

Es gibt ...   There is ...

Ich habe ...   I have ..

Wir haben ... We have ...

To say what there is for people to do there, a great starter is:

Man kann ...

This is used to mean all of these things: You can ... One can ... They can ... We can ...

However, it is much better to add this little word: *da ...* <u>*Da kann man ...*</u> <u>There</u> you can ...

Here are some examples of how this works:

There, you can ...

Da *kann man schwimmen gehen.*	... go swimming.
Da *kann man einen Ausflug machen.*	... go on a trip.
Da *kann man die Sehenswürdigkeiten besichtigen.*	... go sight-seeing.
Da *kann man einen Einkaufsbummel machen.*	... go on a shopping spree.
Da *kann man in den Bergen wandern.*	... go hill-walking.
Da *kann man eine Radtour machen.*	... go on a cycling tour.
Da *kann man ein Auto mieten.*	... hire a car.

On the other hand, you might want to say what there **isn't** in your area:

Es gibt **keinen** *Bahnhof.*	There isn't a station. (masculine)
Es gibt **keine** *Bowlingbahn.*	There isn't a bowling alley. (feminine)
Es gibt **kein** *Eisstadion.*	There isn't an ice rink. (neuter)

Top Tip

After starting a sentence with one of these phrases, remember to use **den** or **einen** for **masculine** nouns, **die** or **eine** for **feminine** nouns, and **das** or **ein** for **neuter** nouns.

Es gibt **einen** *Dom.*—There's a cathedral.

Ich habe **eine** *Lieblingsdisko.*—I have a favourite disco.

Wir haben **ein** *Einkaufszentrum.*— We have a shopping centre.

See the Grammar section, pages 92–93, for cases.

Extended grammar

You might want to say what there is for different kinds of people to do:

Für ...	for ...	*sportliche Leute*	sporty people
die Einwohner von ...	the residents of ...	*Touristen*	tourists
Jugendliche	teenagers	*Studenten*	students
alte Leute	old people	*Naturfreunde*	nature lovers

es gibt ...	there is / are ...
gute Verkehrsverbindungen	a good public transport service
schöne Grünanlagen	lovely public parks
allerlei Restaurants	all kinds of restaurants
ein modernes Theater	a modern theatre
Studentenkneipen	student pubs
moderne Sportmöglichkeiten	modern sports facilities
gute Einkaufsmöglichkeiten	good shopping facilities

Here are some other ways to suggest things to do:

Wenn man ein tolles Nachtleben möchte ...	If you want a great night life ...
Für Fitnessfanatiker gibt es ...	For fitness fanatics there is / are ...
Wenn man sich erholen will ...	If you want to relax ...
Direkt in der Nähe ist ...	Very close by there is ...
Am interessantesten ist / sind ...	Most interesting of all is / are ...
Es erwarten Sie (viele neue Abenteuer).	(Lots of new adventures) await you.

Top Tip

In *wenn* clauses, which **end** with a verb, the next clause **starts** with a verb, e.g. **Wenn** man ins Konzert gehen **will, haben** wir jeden Freitagabend eine Vorstellung. **Wenn** man Lust auf ein Eis **hat, kann** man ins Eiscafé gehen. **Wenn** ein Fußballspiel im Standion **stattfindet, kommen** tausende von Fans.

Quick Test

Translate the following sentences into English:

1 *Man kann in den vielen Grünanlagen joggen gehen.*

2 *Direkt in der Nähe ist ein fantastischer Musikladen.*

3 *Das Hotel liegt in einer ruhigen Lage.*

4 *Da kann man sich gut erholen.*

Extended vocabulary 1

Home

Wir wohnen in ...	We live in ...
einer ruhigen Lage	a quiet spot
einem kleinen Vorort	a small suburb
einer lebendigen Gegend	a lively area
einem malerischen Dorf	a picturesque village
einer bequemen Wohnung	a comfortable flat
einem kleinen Dorf	a little village
einem Vorort von ( )	in a suburb of ( )
Im Garten haben wir ...	In the garden we have ...
Blumenbeete	flowerbeds
Gartenstühle	garden chairs
einen Gartentisch	a garden table
eine Schaukel	a swing
einen Schuppen	a shed
einen Teich	a pond
eine Terrasse	a patio
eine Hecke	a hedge
einige Bäume	some trees
Rosensträucher	rose bushes
einen Rasen	a lawn
einen Zaun	a fence

N.B. The preposition in the DATIVE case is used if there is no movement from one place to another.

Das ist ...	It's ...
ein modernes Gebäude	a modern building
ein stinknormales Gebäude	a bog standard building
Das ist eine ...	It's a ...
lebendige ...	lively ...
schöne ...	beautiful ...
Gegend	area

Top Tip

Choose some phrases you think will suit, and learn to use them accurately. Avoid simply writing a list of things.

Quick Test

Write a brochure for your ideal place to live. What information could you give about the facilities and entertainments for people of all ages and interests?

Try to vary the stuctures you use. Don't use *es gibt* all the time!

Extended vocabulary 2

Living room

Unser Wohnzimmer ist ...	our living room is ...
recht gemütlich	really cosy
sehr bequem	very comfortable
Wir haben ...	We have ...
ein Ledersofa	a leather sofa
zwei Sessel	two armchairs
einen Kaffeetisch	a coffee table
einen Fernseher	a television
einen DVD-Player	a DVD player
eine Stehlampe	a standard lamp
ein Bücherregal	a bookcase
einen Kamin	a fireplace
einige Lampen	some lamps
einen grünen Teppich	a green carpet
einen großen Spiegel	a big mirror
einige Topfpflanzen	some pot plants
weiße Gardinen	white curtains
ein paar Bilder an den Wänden	a few pictures on the walls
Da ist es sehr gemütlich.	It's very cosy there.
Abends ...	In the evenings ...
sehen wir fern	we watch TV
plaudern wir	we chat
spielen wir Karten	we play cards
besprechen wir was tagsüber geschehen ist	we talk about what's happened during the day
spielen wir mit dem Hund / der Katze	we play with the dog /cat
ruhen wir uns aus	we relax

Quick Test

Choose something from the list on the right for each of these groups of people to do:

1 Für Fitnessfanatiker gibt es ...　　　　a schöne Grünanlagen

2 Für Touristen gibt es ...　　　　b fantastische Eikaufsmöglichkeiten

3 Für Jugendliche gibt es ...　　　　c mehrere Kinos

4 Für Naturfreunde gibt es ...　　　　d ein modernes Stadion

5 Für Filmfanatiker gibt es ...　　　　e einen Fitnessraum

6 Für Studenten gibt es ...　　　　f einen Jugendklub

7 Für Mädchen und Frauen gibt es ...　　　　g Studentenkneipen

8 Für Fußballfans gibt es ...　　　　h gute Hotels

Where I live 3

Exercise 1

6

Here is Ralf describing his home town. Listen and choose the correct word each time.

Wir wohnen in einem mittelgroßen <u>Doppelhaus</u> / <u>Reihenhaus</u> in einer kleinen Straße, <u>nicht weit von</u> / <u>in der Nähe von</u> der Stadtmitte. Hier gefällt es mir sehr gut, weil wir in einer <u>lebendigen</u> / <u>ruhigen</u> Gegend wohnen. Mein Schlafzimmer ist im <u>Erdgeschoss</u> / <u>ersten Stock</u> und von meinem Fenster habe ich einen schönen Blick auf den Garten. Da gibt es <u>einen Rasen</u> / <u>eine Terrasse</u>, wo wir im Sommer <u>sitzen</u> / <u>grillen</u>. In meinem Zimmer habe ich <u>einen Schreibtisch</u> / <u>einen Computertisch</u>, wo ich <u>Hausaufgaben mache</u> / <u>am Computer spiele</u>. <u>Auf dem Schrank</u> / <u>Boden</u> ist meine CD Sammlung, und an den Wänden hängen <u>viele Fotos</u> / <u>viele Poster</u> von Tieren. Wenn ich <u>in den Bergen</u> / <u>auf dem Land</u> wandern gehe, nehme ich immer meinen Fotoapparat mit.

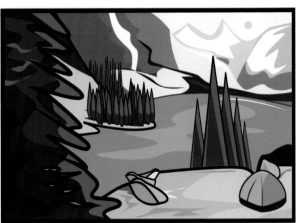

Extended vocabulary 3

In der Gegend gibt es ...	In the area, there are / is ...	*Straßencafés*	street cafés
		Touristen	tourists
Berge	mountains		
einen Fluß	a river	*Wir haben viel ...*	We have a lot of ...
einen See	a lake	*Verkehr*	traffic
einen Wald	a forest		
		Die Leute sind ...	The people are ...
Wir haben viele ...	We have a lot of ...	*fies*	horrible
Autos	cars	*freundlich*	friendly
Fußgängerzonen	pedestrian areas	*gastfreundlich*	hospitable
Kinderspielplätze	children's playgrounds	*hilfsbereit*	helpful
		stur	dour
Parkanlagen	parks	*sympathisch*	nice

Top Tip
Always have a look at the task or questions **before** you listen to a passage. This will help you to concentrate on the essential information that you will need to answer accurately.

Top Tip
Exclamations such as the following make your spoken German in particular sound more fluent:
Alles klar! – That's fine!
Weißt du ... – You know ...
Toll! – Great!
In Ordnung – Sorted!
Mensch! – Wow!

Exercise 2 7

Listen to and read through this phone conversation. Craig is about to visit his penfriend Birte for the first time in Munich.

B   Hallo Craig. Vater und ich holen dich vom Flughafen ab.

C   Danke, Birte. Wohnst du in der Nähe vom Flughafen?

B   Eigentlich nicht – unsere Wohnung liegt südlich vom Flughafen, eine Dreiviertelstunde mit dem Auto.

C   Alles klar. Und was machen wir in der nächsten Woche?

B   Also, ich habe uns Karten für das Fußballspiel am Samstag besorgt – Bayern München gegen Werder Bremen. Das Spiel findet in der Allianz Arena statt. Das ist ein tolles modernes Stadion.

C   Super! Und wie kommen wir zur Allianz Arena?

B   Weißt du, die U-Bahnstation ist direkt in der Nähe von unserem Haus, und die Linie 6 fährt zum Stadion.

C   Toll! Ich freue mich darauf. Was gibt es in München zu sehen und zu tun?

B   Wenn du Lust hast, können wir den Olympiaturm besichtigen. Von da oben hat man einen fantastischen Blick auf die Stadt. Und die BMW Fabrik liegt neben dem Turm.

C   In Ordnung! Und was für Sehenswürdigkeiten gibt es noch in München?

B   Na, das Rathaus ist berühmt. Jeden Tag kommen hunderte von Touristen, um es zu sehen. Da gehen wir auch hin. Und gleich in der Nähe ist der Viktualienmarkt. Das ist ein großer Markt, wo man nicht nur allerlei Obst, Gemüse, Wurst und Brot kaufen kann, sondern auch jede Menge Souvenirs und Postkarten.

C   Oh, ich möchte eine Postkarte von dem fabelhaften Schloss kaufen. Wie heißt es noch?

B   Meinst du Schloss Neuschwanstein? Ja, das müssen wir unbedingt sehen.

C   Mensch, ich kann es kaum er warten. Wir sehen uns also am Donnerstag. Bis dann!

B   Ja, Tschüs! – bis Donnerstag, Craig!

Exercise 3

Tick the town features below if they are in Munich and cross if they are not.

	Yes	No
1 Fairground	☐	☐
2 Car factory	☐	☐
3 Airport	☐	☐
4 Ice rink	☐	☐
5 Market	☐	☐
6 Multiplex	☐	☐
7 Town hall	☐	☐

Quick Test

Find the German in the text for:

1 I'm looking forward to it.
2 We've definitely got to see that.
3 Three quarters of an hour
4 From the top …
5 Lots of souvenirs and postcards

Transport 1

Basic vocabulary

Types of transport

Ich fahre …	I travel …
mit dem Bus	by bus
mit dem Zug	by train
mit dem Auto	by car
mit dem Mofa	by moped
mit dem Motorrad	by motor bike
mit dem Schiff	by ship
mit der Bahn	by rail
mit der Fähre	by ferry
mit der S-Bahn	by local train
mit der Straßenbahn	by tram
mit der U-Bahn	by underground

Bus / underground

der Busbahnhof	bus station
die Bushaltestelle	bus stop
die Fahrkarte	ticket
die Linie (5)	(bus) number (5)
die S-Bahnstation	local train station
die Straßenbahnhaltestelle	tram stop
die U-Bahnstation	underground station

Train

einfach	single
hin- und zurück	return
der Fahrkartenautomat	ticket machine
der Schalter	ticket office
die Auskunft	information
der Gleis	track
der Bahnsteig	platform
der Bahnhof	station

Top Tip

In English we say that the train is at Platform 12, but in German we have to say the train is on Track 12: *Der Zug ist auf Gleis 12.* The platform (*der Bahnsteig*) is strictly for passengers!

der Hauptbahnhof	main station
die Deutsche Bundesbahn (DB)	German Federal Railways
der Warteraum	waiting room
Abfahrt	departures
Ankunft	arrivals
der Eingang	entrance
der Ausgang	exit
der Fahrplan	timetable
Raucher	smoking
Nichtraucher	non-smoking
der Platz	seat
die Fahrgäste	passengers
der Zug hat 5 Minuten Verspätung	the train is 5 minutes late

Plane

die Abfertigung	check-in
der Abflug	take-off
der Eingang	entrance
der Flughafen	airport
das Flugzeug / die Maschine	aeroplane
der Flug	flight
die Fluggäste	airline passengers
das Gepäck	luggage
der Koffer	suitcase
die Kofferkulis	trolleys
der Reisepass	passport
das Schild	sign
der Zoll	customs
der Zollbeamte	customs officer

Car

der Vordersitz	front seat
der Rücksitz	back seat
der Motor	engine
die Bremsen	brakes
eine Panne	breakdown
die Reifen	tyres
die Reifenpanne	flat tyre
die Windschutzscheibe	windscreen
die Scheibenwischer	windscreen-wipers
die Scheinwerfer	headlights
das Lenkrad	steering wheel

Extended vocabulary 1

Bus

Wo ist die Bushaltestelle?	Where is the bus stop?
Wann fährt der nächste / letzte Bus nach ...?	When is the next / last bus to ...?
Wie oft fährt der Bus?	How often do the buses run?
Fährt dieser Bus Richtung Zoo?	Is this the right bus for the zoo?
Welche Linie fährt zum Dom?	Which bus goes to the cathedral?
Steigen Sie am Marktplatz aus.	Get off at the market square.

Train

Ich möchte ...	I would like ...
zweimal einfach nach ...	two singles to ...
einmal hin- und zurück nach ...	one return to ...
erster Klasse	first class
zweiter Klasse	second class
Raucher	smoking
Nichtraucher	non-smoking
der Zug aus Hamburg	the train from Hamburg
Wann fährt der Zug nach Kiel ab?	When does the train to Kiel leave?
Wann kommt der Zug in Köln an?	When does the train arrive in Cologne?
Muss ich umsteigen?	Do I have to change?
Von welchem Gleis fährt der Zug?	Which track (platform) does the train leave from?

Top Tip
Travelling by: When using **masculine** or **neuter** nouns, use *mit dem*. When using **feminine** nouns, use *mit der*. See the Grammar section, pages 92–93, on cases.

Extended vocabulary 2

Plane

Wo muss ich einchecken?	Where do I have to check in?
Ich habe nur einen Koffer	I only have one suitcase
... und ein Stück Handgepäck	... and one piece of hand luggage
Wo sind die Kofferkulis?	Where are the trolleys?
Ich habe meine Flugkarte verloren	I've lost my ticket
Ich habe nichts zu verzollen	I've nothing to declare
Gibt es eine Busverbindung in die Stadtmitte?	Is there a bus service to the town centre?

Driving

die Autobahn	motorway
die Bundesstraße	'A' road
die Landstraße	'B' road
die Ausfahrt	slip road off
die Einfahrt	slip road on
die Umleitung	diversion
die Raststätte	service station
das Benzin	petrol
der Diesel	diesel
der Luftdruck	air pressure
die Tankstelle	filling station
die Reparaturwerkstatt	repair workshop
die Einbahnstraße	one-way street
Ich habe eine Panne!	I've broken down!

Quick Test

Find and write out the German for:

1 ticket machine

2 monthly season ticket

3 a breakdown

4 a passport

5 passengers

Transport 2

Basic grammar

When talking about **travelling**, the verb most commonly used is **fahren**.
Remember, this is an **irregular** verb:

Ich fahre	*wir fahren*
*du **fährst***	*ihr fahrt*
*er **fährt***	*Sie fahren*
*sie **fährt***	*sie fahren*
*man **fährt***	

N.B. This is the Present Tense of the verb **fahren**. See the
Grammar section, pages 97–98, for more on irregular verbs.

Top Tip
Other useful verbs
to use in the context
of travelling are:
einsteigen – to get on
aussteigen – to get off
umsteigen – to change
reisen – to travel.

To talk about flying, use the regular
verb **fliegen**. Using time phrases helps you
to put your story in sequence, but remember to
use **inversion** after starting a sentence with a
time phrase:

Jeden Tag *fährt Hans mit dem Bus zur Schule.*	**Every day** Hans goes to school by bus.
Zweimal in der Woche *fahre ich mit dem Zug.*	I travel by train **twice a week**.
Ab und zu *fährt mein Vater Rad.*	My father cycles **now and again**.
In den Ferien *fahren die Kinder Skateboard.*	The children go skateboarding **in the holidays**.
Im Winter *fahren wir Ski.*	**In the winter** we go skiing.
Dann *fliegen wir nach Hause.*	**Then** we fly home.

Other useful phrases

von Glasgow nach München	from Glasgow to Munich
über London	via London

Extended Grammar

If you are describing journeys that you have done in the past, you will need to use the Perfect Tense for events and single completed actions. Remember, the verb **fahren** takes **sein** in the Perfect Tense:

ich **bin** gefahren	Sie **sind** gefahren
du **bist** gefahren	ihr **seid** gefahren
er / sie / es / man **ist** gefahren	sie **sind** gefahren
wir **sind** gefahren	

Top Tip
When there is a mention of **when** something was done, **how** it was done and **where** it was done, these elements have to come in this order. It is called **time – manner – place**.

See the Grammar section, page 98, for verbs taking **sein** in the Perfect Tense.

letztes Jahr	last year	bin ich }	I }
letzten August	last August	sind wir }	we }
in den Osterferien	in the Easter holidays	nach Spanien gefahren	went to Spain

To say **how** you travelled:

*Letztes Jahr bin ich **mit dem Auto** nach England gefahren.* – Last year I went to England **by car**.
*In den Weihnachtsferien sind wir **mit der Fähre** nach Irland gefahren.*
In the Christmas holidays we went to Ireland **by ferry**.
*Im Oktober bin ich **mit dem Zug** nach Paris gefahren.* – In October I went to Paris **by train**.

To say that you flew:

*Wir **sind** nach Kanada **geflogen**.*	We flew to Canada.
*Ich **bin** nach Berlin **geflogen**.*	I flew to Berlin.

To describe how the journey was, use the Imperfect Tense:

*Die Reise **war** …*	The journey **was** …
anstrengend	tiring
lang	long
unbequem	uncomfortable

See the Grammar section, pages 100–101, for the Imperfect Tense.

Quick Test

Write a postcard to your German penfriend, describing your journey when you went on holiday with your family by car all the way to Spain.

Quick Test

Read this postcard and answer the questions that follow:

1 How did they travel to Cologne?
2 Where did they break their journey?
3 Who is Katharina with?
4 What did they do on Wednesday?

Liebe Oma,
Nach einer langen Busreise sind wir rechtzeitig am Montag in Köln angekommen. Wir sind mit der Fähre über Zeebrugge gefahren, wo einige meiner Klassenkameraden Schokolade gekauft haben. Am Mittwoch sind wir mit dem Schiff auf dem Rhein gefahren. Grüße und Küsse,

Katharina

Transport 3

Exercise 1

Label as many things as you can in this picture of a German airport.

_____   _____

_____   _____

_____   _____

_____   _____

_____   _____

_____   _____

_____   _____

_____   _____

_____   _____

Exercise 2

Rearrange these German transport words, then translate them into English.

Anagrams	German	English
ANOBHBUFSH		
FUNKATUS		
CHRÄLIBECESFH		
ENAFFHULG		
MEEBNSR		
GRUNTHIC		
DEHÄKGANCP		
UEMUGLNIT		
TRUCKLFDU		

Exercise 3

Here is an excerpt from the radio travel news.

Listen to each piece of information three times and then write down everything you have understood.

First of all, listen with the book closed, and then listen again with your book open, after you have written down your answers.

1 Wegen einer Panne gibt es einen Stau auf der Autobahn Richtung Bonn.
2 Fahrgäste, die mit dem Zehnuhrbus nach Jena fahren, müssen in Weimar umsteigen.
3 Der Lufthansa Flug 765 nach New York hat drei Stunden Verspätung.
4 Die Autobahn A6 ist wegen Glatteis südlich von Hannover gesperrt.
5 Heute gibt es eine Umleitung über Klausdorf.
6 Weil Karneval in der Stadtmitte ist, fahren die letzten Busse erst um ein Uhr dreißig ab.

Quick Test

By car, bus, train or plane? Decide for each one.

1 Schau mal! Da ist die Ausfahrt Hannover-West.
2 Einmal zum Sportstadion, einfach bitte.
3 Vor dem Abflug muss man den Sicherheitsgurt anschnallen.
4 Wir fahren von Gleis 10 ab.
5 Haben Sie eine Panne? Nein, ich habe kein Benzin mehr.
6 Dreimal hin- und zurück nach Salzburg, erster Klasse, bitte.

Holidays 1

Basic vocabulary

Types of holiday

der Aufenthalt	a stay / visit
die Herbstferien	autumn holidays
Karneval	carnival
die Klassenfahrt	school trip
die Osterferien	Easter holidays
die Reise	journey
der Schüleraustausch	school exchange
die Sommerferien	summer holidays
die Weihnachtsferien	Christmas holidays

Types of accommodation

das Wohnmobil	camper van
der Campingbus	camper bus
der Campingplatz	campsite
das Ferienhaus	holiday home
die Ferienwohnung	holiday apartment
die Jugendherberge	youth hostel
das Jugendhotel	youth hotel
die Pension	bed and breakfast
der Wohnwagen	caravan

mit Bad	with bath
mit Dusche	with shower
mit WC	with toilet
mit Balkon	with balcony
mit Fernseher	with TV
mit Frühstück	with breakfast
mit Halbpension	with half-board
mit Vollpension	with full-board

im ersten Stock	on the first floor
im zweiten Stock	on the second floor
der Aufzug	lift
Bedienung inbegriffen	service included

Locations

im Ausland	abroad
in den Bergen	in the mountains
an der Küste	on the coast
auf dem Lande	in the country
an der See	at the seaside

Destinations

in Barcelona in Spanien	in Barcelona in Spain
in Roma in Italien	in Rome in Italy
in Marmaris in der Türkei	in Marmaris in Turkey
in Malia auf Kreta	in Malia on Crete (on an island)
in LA in den Vereinigten Staaten (USA)	in LA in the United States

Hotel

ein Einzelzimmer	a single room
ein Zweibettzimmer	a twin room
ein Doppelzimmer	a double room

Top Tip

Changes can occur because the prepositions *in, an, auf* take the Accusative case if there is movement from one place to another, but the Dative case if there is no movement from one place to another.

I go abroad = *Ich fahre ins Ausland*

We were abroad = *Wir waren im Ausland*

See the Grammar section, pages 92–93, for cases.

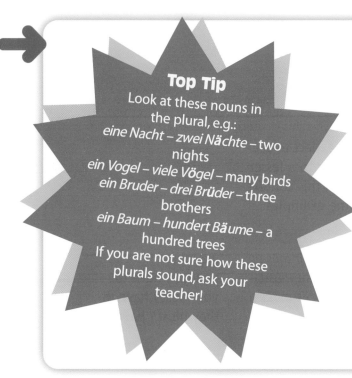

Top Tip

Look at these nouns in the plural, e.g.:
eine Nacht – zwei Nächte – two nights
ein Vogel – viele Vögel – many birds
ein Bruder – drei Brüder – three brothers
ein Baum – hundert Bäume – a hundred trees
If you are not sure how these plurals sound, ask your teacher!

Camping

der Campingplatz	campsite
der Platz	plot / pitch for tent
der Strom	electricity
die Wasserleitung	water supply
die Duschen	showers
die Waschräume	washrooms
die Toiletten	toilets
die Wäscherei	laundry
die Waschmaschine	washing machine
die Mülltonne	rubbish bin
der Spielraum	games room
der Rucksack	rucksack
der Schlafsack	sleeping bag
der Kocher	camping stove
die Streichhölzer	matches
die Taschenlampe	torch
die Gasflasche	gas container

Extended vocabulary

General accommodation phrases

Ich möchte … reservieren	I would like to reserve …
Ich möchte ein Einzelzimmer reservieren.	I would like to reserve a single room.
*Ich möchte ein Doppelzimmer für **eine Nacht** reservieren.*	I would like to reserve a double room for one night.
*Wir möchten ein Zweibettzimmer für **fünf Nächte** reservieren.*	We would like to reserve a twin room for five nights.
Haben Sie Plätze frei?	Do you have any spaces free?
Wie lange wollen Sie bleiben?	How long do you want to stay?
Für drei Nächte.	For three nights.
Für wie viele Personen?	For how many people?
Für zwei Erwachsene und zwei Kinder.	For two adults and two children.
Was kostet das Zimmer?	What does the room cost?
Was kostet das pro Person pro Nacht?	What does it cost per person per night?
Würden Sie bitte dieses Formular ausfüllen?	Would you fill in this form, please?
Gibt es einen Parkplatz?	Is there a car park?
Direkt vor / hinter dem Hotel.	Right in front of / behind the hotel.
Die Lampe funktioniert nicht.	The light isn't working.
Das Wasser ist eiskalt.	The water is freezing.
Die Fernbedienung ist kaputt.	The remote control is broken.
Der Aufzug ist außer Betrieb.	The lift is out of order.

Quick Test

How would you say, or ask for the following?

1 In Porto Pollensa on Majorca.

2 A single room with full board.

3 Is the hotel wheelchair accessible?

Holidays 2

Basic grammar

Rules and regulations

If you are staying in a youth hostel or on a campsite, expect to see some rules and regulations around the place. This is true to a lesser extent in hotels! The important verbs which are used in this context belong to a group called **Modal Verbs**. Here are some examples:

Top Tip
Can and may use different verbs in German: *I can* swim = I am **able** to swim = *Ich kann schwimmen.* **May** I swim in the lake? = Am I **allowed** to swim in the lake? = *Darf ich im See schwimmen?*

müssen – must, have to

ich muss	I must / have to	*wir müssen*	we must / have to
du musst	you must / have to	*ihr müsst*	you (pl.) have to
er / sie / es / man muss	he / she / it / one must / has to	*Sie müssen*	you must / have to
		sie müssen	they must / have to

dürfen – may, be allowed to

ich darf	I may	*wir dürfen*	we may
du darfst	you may	*ihr dürft*	you (pl.) may
er / sie / es / man darf	he / she / it / one may	*Sie dürfen*	you may
		sie dürfen	they may

können – can, able to

ich kann	I can	*wir können*	we can
du kannst	you can	*ihr könnt*	you (pl.) can
er / sie / es / man kann	he / she / it / one can	*Sie können*	you can
		sie können	they can

Some examples of information and regulations

Gäste müssen den Ausweis vorzeigen.	Guests must show their IDs.
Man kann den Schlüssel vom Herbergsvater holen.	One can get the key from the warden.
Kinder ab zwei Jahre dürfen im Planschbecken spielen.	Children over two may play in the paddling pool.
Man muss keine Flaschen oder Gläser ins Schwimmbad bringen.	Bottles and glasses must not be brought to the swimming pool.
Jugendliche unter 16 Jahre dürfen keinen Alkohol kaufen.	Teenagers under 16 are not allowed to purchase alcohol.

Some notices use a more forceful tone!

Rauchen verboten!	No smoking!	*Tauchen strengstens untersagt!*	Strictly no diving!
Kein Zutritt!	No entry!	*Hunde nicht erlaubt!*	Dogs not allowed!
Das Tragen von Wanderschuhen ist im Haus nicht erstattet!		Hiking boots are not to be worn indoors!	

Extended grammar

If you want to write about or talk about holidays you have had, you will need to use the **Perfect Tense**. See page 98 for more on the Perfect Tense.

Here are some things you might say about a holiday in the past (using **haben** verbs):

Ich **habe** }
               } *die Sehenswürdigkeiten* **besichtigt**.
Wir **haben** }

        I / we visited the sights.

Ich **habe** }
               } *zwei Wochen in der Schweiz* **verbracht**.
Wir **haben** }

        I / we spent two weeks in Switzerland.

Ich **habe** }
               } *viele Fotos* **gemacht**.
Wir **haben** }

        I / we took lots of photos.

> **Top Tip**
> To say where you **stayed** on holiday, the verb **wohnen** must be used, e.g. *Wir haben in einem Hotel gewohnt.* – We **stayed** in a hotel. *Sie haben auf einem Campingplatz gewohnt.* – They **stayed** on a campsite.

Some verbs use **sein** in the Perfect Tense.

*Wir **sind** jeden Tag schwimmen gegangen.*　　　We went swimming every day.
*Mein Bruder **ist** den ganzen Tag am Strand geblieben.*　　　My brother stayed on the beach all day.
*Ich **bin** nach Athen geflogen.*　　　I flew to Athens.

How would you describe your holiday?

Das Hotel **war** …	The hotel was …
echt toll!	brilliant!
zentral gelegen	right in the centre
heruntergekommen	dilapidated

Die Leute waren …	The people were …
gastfreundlich	hospitable
hilfsbereit	helpful
sympathisch	nice

Quick Test

Translate the following sentences into English:

1 *Wir haben ein Doppelzimmer mit WC und Dusche reserviert.*

2 *Haben Sie Plätze für ein Zelt und einen Campingbus frei?*

3 *Ihr müsst Laken oder Schlafsäcke mitbringen.*

4 *Hunde dürfen nicht ins Hotel kommen.*

Exercise 1

You have a summer job on a German campsite. Make a sign to inform the campers what they can and cannot do.

Holidays 3

Exercise 1

Here is a conversation between a campsite manager and a tourist who has just arrived with his family. Can you put the dialogue into the correct order?

Manager

- *Haben Sie eine Taschenlampe dabei?*
- *€15 pro Person pro Nacht.*
- *Guten Abend. Haben Sie reserviert?*
- *Ja, wir haben einen Wäscheraum. Ihr Zeltplatz ist links vom Wäscheraum.*
- *Das können Sie im Supermarkt kaufen. Er ist bis 22.00 Uhr geöffnet.*
- *Für wie viele Personen?*
- *Es tut mir leid. Das ist der letzte Platz. Es ist ja 21.00 Uhr!*
- *Ja, ich habe einen Platz. Für wie viele Nächte?*

Tourist

- *Für fünf Nächte. Was kostet das?*
- *Ja, ich weiß – wir sind sehr spät angekommen, und es ist dunkel.*
- *Das ist aber teuer! Na gut! Gibt es hier einen Wäscheraum? Unsere Kleider sind schmutzig.*
- *Dann gehe ich gleich hin.*
- *Nein, wir haben nicht reserviert. Haben Sie noch Platz frei?*
- *Aber das finde ich zu laut. Haben Sie andere Zeltplätze?*
- *Zwei Erwachsene und drei Kinder.*
- *Ja danke, das habe ich – aber ich brauche eine Flasche Gas.*

Exercise 2

CREDIT

Max Meier, the manager of the youth hotel in Munich, is giving his welcome talk to a newly arrived school group from Dundee. Listen and read.

Hallo Leute, und herzlich willkommen im Jugendhotel Scala. Mein Name ist Max Meier, und ich bin der Manager von diesem Hotel. Erst mal ein paar Tips, damit wir miteinander gut auskommen.

Erstens müssen alle Gäste ein Anmeldeformular ausfüllen. Die könnt ihr beim Empfang holen.

Bitte achtet darauf, dass man keine Getränke und kein Fast-Food in die Schlafzimmer bringen darf. Ab elf Uhr abends ist Nachtruhe. Das heißt, dass laute Musik strengstens untersagt ist, und ihr dürft nicht in der Nähe der Schlafzimmer schreien, laut singen oder Lärm machen.

Wichtig ist auch, dass man weiß, dass hier im ganzen Hotel das Rauchen verboten ist – sowohl in den Schlafzimmern wie auch hier im Erdgeschoss.

Direkt hinter dem Hotel haben wir ein tolles Freibad für unsere Gäste. Ihr dürft das Schwimmbad von 7.00 Uhr bis 20.00 Uhr benutzen – das heißt, man kann den ganzen Tag schwimmen gehen. Ab 20.00 Uhr aber ist kein Zutritt mehr, und Schwimmen ist nicht erlaubt.

Wenn ihr ein Fahrrad mieten möchtet, könnt ihr das beim Empfang bezahlen. Aber nicht vergessen – ihr müsst die Fahrräder bis spätestens 21.00 Uhr zurückgeben.

Bei Feueralarm darf man den Aufzug nicht betreten. Das ist ja gefährlich! In dem Fall, müsst ihr die Treppe nehmen.

Das Frühstück wird von 6.30 bis 9.30 Uhr serviert und das Abendessen von 18 Uhr bis 20.00 Uhr. Gäste müssen den Ausweis vorzeigen, wenn sie den Speisesaal betreten.

Zum Schluss wünsche ich euch einen angenehmen Aufenthalt bei uns hier im Jugendhotel Scala!

Quick Test

Draw three columns on a sheet. At the top of the left-hand column, put the heading '**Do's**', above the middle one '**Must's**' and above the right hand one, '**Don'ts**'.

Now look at the text above while listening to the CD again, and fill in the appropriate column with things you may do, must do and things you may not do.

Eating out 1

Basic vocabulary

Cold drinks

kalte Getränke	cold drinks
das Mineralwasser	mineral water
der Sprudel	fizzy water
die Limonade (Limo)	lemonade
die Cola	Coke
Cola Light	diet Coke
der Eiskaffee	iced coffee
der Orangensaft	orange juice
der Apfelsaft	apple juice
die Milch	milk
die Schokomilch	chocolate milk

Hot drinks

heiße Getränke	hot drinks
der Kaffee	coffee
der Milchkaffee	white coffee
der Tee mit Milch	tea with milk
der Tee mit Zitrone	tea with lemon
die heiße Schokolade	hot chocolate
der Kakao	cocoa

Alcoholic drinks

alkoholische Getränke	alcoholic drinks
das Bier	beer
das Hellbier	light beer
das Dunkelbier	dark beer
der Radler	shandy
der Weißwein	white wine
der Rotwein	red wine
der Sekt	sparkling wine

Snacks

die Brezel	pretzel
das belegte Brötchen	filled roll
das Käsebrot	cheese sandwich
das Schinkenbrot	ham sandwich
die Bockwurst	hot dog type sausage
die Bratwurst	fried sausage
die Currywurst	curried sausage
die Pizza	pizza
die Pommes frites	chips

Top Tip

When ordering a snack, you can use:
Ich möchte ... or ich hätte gern – I would like ...
and then:
ein*mal* Apfelsaft – **one** apple juice
zwei*mal* Sprudel – **two** fizzy waters
drei*mal* Currywurst – **three** curried sausages

Pommes mit Mayo	chips with mayonnaise
das Eis	ice cream
eine Kugel . . .	one scoop of ...
zwei Kugel . . .	two scoops of ...
Vanilleeis	vanilla ice cream
Schokoladeneis	chocolate ice cream

Top Tip

When going into a *Konditorei* (cake shop / café), tell the assistant which cake you would like from the display counter, and they will give you a ticket. Sit down at your table, and when they come to take your order, give them the ticket, and they will bring it to you from the counter.

Extended vocabulary

Restaurant dishes

Vorspeisen	**Starters**
die Tagessuppe	soup of the day
die Hühnersuppe	chicken soup
die Tomatensuppe	tomato soup
der Räucherlachs	smoked salmon

Top Tip

When you want to catch a waiter's attention, call 'Herr Ober'. For a waitress, call 'Fräulein!' When you want to pay, say 'Zahlen, bitte!'

Hauptgerichte	**Main courses**
Wiener Schnitzel	veal or pork escalope
Brathähnchen	roast chicken
Eisbein mit Sauerkraut	knuckle of pork with pickled cabbage
Zwei Spiegeleier	two fried eggs
Schinkenomelett	ham omelette
Champignonomelett	mushroom omelette
Backfisch	fried fish
Forelle	trout
Seezunge mit Kräuterbutter	lemon sole with herb butter
Meeresfrüchte	seafood
Matjes Heringe	pickled herring

Gemüse und Salate	**Vegetables and salads**
grüner Salat	green salad
gemischter Salat	mixed salad
Gurkensalat	cucumber salad
Kartoffelsalat	potato salad
Kartoffeln	potatoes
Bratkartoffeln	fried potatoes
Salzkartoffeln	boiled potatoes
Erbsen	peas
grüne Bohnen	French beans
Karotten	carrots
Blumenkohl	cauliflower
Spargel je nach Saison	asparagus when in season
Reis	rice
Nudeln	pasta

Nachspeisen	**Desserts**
Himbeeren	raspberries
Erdbeeren mit Schlagsahne	strawberries with whipped cream
Obstsalat	fruit salad
Quark mit Waldfrüchten	quark with fruits of the forest
Joghurt	yoghurt
der Eisbecher	ice cream sundae

Kuchen	**Cakes**
die Schwarzwälderkirschtorte	Black Forest gateau
die Obsttorte	fruit flan
die Schokoladentorte	chocolate cake
die Mokkatorte	coffee gateau
die Käsesahnetorte	cheesecake
der Streuselkuchen	cake with a crumble topping
der Apfelkuchen	apple cake
… mit Sahne	… with cream
MWS inbegriffen	VAT included
Bedienung inbegriffen	service included

Quick Test

Draw two columns and put each of the following foods into one of these categories: **gesund** for healthy food and **ungesund** for not so healthy food.

- Gurkensalat
- Backfisch mit Pommes frites
- Käsesahnetorte mit Schlagsahne
- Drei Kugel Schokoladeneis mit Sahne
- Forelle
- Salzkartoffeln
- Apfelkuchen
- gemischter Salat

Eating out 2

Essential conversation phrases

Arriving and ordering

Haben Sie einen Tisch frei?	Do you have a table free?
Wie viele sind Sie?	For how many people?
Wir sind drei.	There are three of us.
Leider nicht.	I'm afraid not.
Wir sind völlig ausgebucht	We're completely booked up.
Ja, wir haben einen Fenstertisch.	Yes, we have a table at the window.
Raucher oder Nichtraucher?	Smoking or non-smoking?
Ich möchte die Speisekarte sehen.	I would like to see the menu.
Was können Sie empfehlen?	What can you recommend?
Was ist der Tagessgericht?	What is the dish of the day?
Möchten Sie gleich bestellen?	Would you like to order now?
Haben Sie bestellt?	Have you ordered?
Was darf es sein?	What would you like?
Sonst noch etwas?	Anything else?
Nein, danke! Das ist alles.	No thanks, that's all.
Haben Sie vegetarische Gerichte?	Do you have vegetarian dishes?
Ich bin Vegetarier / Vegetarierin.	I'm a vegetarian.
Wir haben eine große Auswahl.	We have a large selection.
Ich nehme die Spiegeleier.	I'll have the fried eggs.
Für mich die Krabben.	The prawns for me.
Es tut mir leid – der Schweinebraten ist aus.	Sorry, the roast pork's off the menu.
Was trinken Sie dazu?	What would you like to drink with that?
Ich trinke ein Mineralwasser dazu.	I'll have a mineral water with that.
Noch etwas Wasser, bitte.	Some more water, please.
Ist alles in Ordnung?	Is everything all right?
Was möchten Sie als Nachtisch?	What would you like for dessert?
Ich möchte bitte zahlen!	I'd like the bill, please!
Ist Bedienung inbegriffen?	Is service included?
das Trinkgeld	tip
Schönen Abend noch!	Have a nice evening!

Top Tip

You probably know that it is customary to say *Bitte!* or *Bitte schön!* when somebody thanks you in German. However, when the waitress brings your order, she will probably say: *So, bitte schön!* – which means *There you are!* If you want to say *Yes please!* just say *Ja, bitte!* or *Bitte!* If you want to say *No thank you!* just say *Nein, danke!* or *Danke!*

Problems

Wir warten schon seit 30 Minuten.*	We've been waiting 30 minutes.
Das habe ich nicht bestellt!	I didn't order that!
Wir haben keine Pizza bestellt.	We didn't order pizza.
Dieses Gericht ist kalt.	This dish is cold.
Das Glas ist schmutzig.	The glass is dirty.
Mir fehlt ein Messer / eine Gabel / ein Löffel.	I'm missing a knife / fork / spoon.
Man hat einen Fehler gemacht.	There's been a mistake.
Ich möchte den Manager sprechen.**	I'd like to speak to the manager.
Ich möchte mich beschweren.	I would like to complain.
Das schmeckt fürchterlich.	That tastes terrible.
Die Currywurst ist zu scharf.	The curry sauce is too spicy.
Die Rechnung ist falsch.	The bill is wrong.

* When saying that something **has been done** for a certain amount of time, the present tense is used with **seit**, e.g. 'Ich lerne deutsch <u>seit</u> vier Jahren' = 'I have been learning German for four years'.

** This is in the **Conditional = I would like**.

Exercise 1

Which of the above complaints are in the Present Tense, and which are in the Perfect Tense? Make two lists, one headed Present, and one headed Perfect.

Quick Test

Can you decide whether it is the customer **(C)** or the waitress **(W)** speaking? Then translate these sentences into English:

1 Haben Sie schon bestellt?

2 Was können Sie empfehlen?

3 Ich möchte die Speisekarte sehen.

4 Wieviele sind Sie?

5 Die Gabel ist schmutzig.

6 Ich trinke eine Cola dazu.

7 Ich habe keine Cola bestellt.

8 Was darf es sein?

9 Schönen Tag noch!

10 Ich bin allergisch gegen Käse.

Eating out 3

Exercise 1

Work out these German anagrams of food and drink items. Next learn the German words. Finally, try translating them into English.

Anagrams	German	English
DRINKS		
DESRULP		
OKAKA		
FETSLAPFA		
HEKIFLCEMAF		
DILANOEM		
FOODS		
MESPMO TRESFI		
EGRISEPLEIE		
ROLTARFAKEFTNB		
TOSTERBOT		
BENESR		
REMIHENEB		

Exercise 2

10 ⊂⊃

You go into a restaurant in Freiburg for lunch. Read and listen to what the waiter says and give a suitable reply.

1 *Wie viele sind Sie?*

2 *Raucher oder Nichtraucher?*

3 *Möchten Sie die Speisekarte sehen?*

4 *Was darf es sein?*

5 *Sind Sie Vegetarier?*

6 *Was trinken Sie dazu?*

7 *Ist alles in Ordnung?*

8 *Schönen Tag noch!*

Exercise 3

Listen to these five orders without looking at the text below. Give details of the order and the total bill for each table.

Once you have written your answers, refer to the text below to check them.

1 *Die alten Damen am Tisch Nummer vierzehn: Einmal Schwarzwälderkirschtorte, einmal Apfelkuchen mit Schlagsahne und zweimal Milchkaffee. Zwölf Euro vierzig.*

2 *Die Kinder am Tisch Nummer dreizehn: Einmal Cola, einmal Sprudel, einmal Erdbeereis, einmal Eisbecher. Neun Euro fünfundsechzig.*

3 *Tisch Nummer elf: Zweimal Käseomelett mit Bratkartoffeln, einmal Apfelsaft und einmal Orangensaft. Elf Euro neunzig.*

4 *Die Schotten am Tisch Nummer sechs: Dreimal Backfisch mit Pommes, und einmal Wiener Schnitzel. Neunzehn Euro fünfundzwanzig.*

5 *Also, Tisch Nummer sieben: Einmal Bockwurst mit Kartoffelsalat, einmal Jägerschnitzel mit Salzkartoffeln und zweimal gemischter Salat. Macht zusammen sechzehn Euro fünfundvierzig.*

Top Tip

When ordering more than one of any food or drink, do not use the plural of that food or drink:

Zwiemal Forelle
Viermal Mokkatorte

Quick Test

Put these café orders into German:

1 One ham roll and one fizzy water.

2 Two portions of chips with mayonnaise and two coffees.

3 Three Cokes and three lemon teas.

4 One chocolate cake and one ice cream: strawberry and vanilla.

5 One ice cream sundae and one curry sausage.

6 One fruit flan with whipped cream and one tea with milk.

Relationships 1

Basic vocabulary

Positive qualities

nett	nice
lieb	nice / kind
freundlich	friendly
ruhig	quiet
süß	sweet
toll	fabulous
lebhaft	lively
kontaktfreudig	outgoing
temperamentvoll	vivacious
vernünftig	sensible
selbstständig	independent
extravagant	flamboyant
zuverlässig	reliable
zurückhaltend	reserved
geduldig	patient
treu	loyal
großzügig	generous
verständnisvoll	understanding
lustig	funny
bescheiden	modest
schüchtern	shy
extravert	extrovert
ehrlich	honest
liebenswürdig	kind
organisiert	organised
höflich	polite
sensibel	sensitive
charmant	charming
hilsbereit	helpful
reif	mature
gehorsam	obedient
schwatzhaft	chatty
fleißig	hard working
ernst	serious
aufgeschlossen	open-minded
sympathisch	nice / pleasant

Negative qualities

aggressiv	aggressive
egoistisch	selfish
arrogant	arrogant
brummig / grantig	moany
anstrengend	demanding
deprimierend	depressing
unehrlich	dishonest
verklemmt	inhibited
verantwortungslos	irresponsible
geizig	mean (with money)
gemein	mean (spirited)
verschlossen	withdrawn
unverschämt	outrageous
schmuddelig	messy / sloppy
boshaft	nasty / malicious
nervig	annoying
ärgerlich	irritating
ekelhaft	horrible
asozial	antisocial
faul	lazy
ungeduldig	impatient
eifersüchtig	envious
doof	daft
blöd	silly
dumm	stupid
angespannt	uptight
langweilig	boring

Extended vocabulary

CREDIT

How we get on ... or not!

Wir kommen miteinander gut aus.	We get on well.
Wir verstehen uns gut.	We get on well.
Wir vertragen uns gut.	We get on well.
Wir haben nie Streit.	We never argue.
Wir streiten uns selten.	We rarely argue.
Wir haben viel gemeinsam.	We have lots in common.
Wir machen viel zusammen.	We do a lot together.
Wir kommen miteinander nicht gut aus.	We don't get on well.
Wir verstehen uns nicht gut.	We get on badly.
Wir vertragen uns nicht gut.	We can't bear each other.
Wir haben oft Streit.	We often have arguments.
Wir streiten uns oft.	We often argue.
Wir haben nichts gemeinsam.	We have nothing in common.
Wir unternehmen wenig zusammen.	We do very little together.

Top Tip

Sometimes, you can extend your sentences by using conjunctions which **do not** cause the word order to be altered such as *und* (and), *aber* (but), *oder* (or) or *denn* (because)...

Quick Test

1 Write out a phrase detailing how you get on with each member of your family.

You can change from the *wir* to the *ich* form of the verb; remember, though, that when you use the preposition *mit* you have to put the next word into the dative case (see pages 94–96 of the Grammar section for further information).

e.g. *Ich komme mit meinem Vater sehr gut aus.*   I get on well with my father.

or

Meine Oma und ich vertragen uns gut.   My gran and I get on well.

2 Taking each of your friends in turn, write a sentence to describe them:

e.g. *Isobel ist sympathisch und treu.*

    Kenny ist lustig und großzügig.

Do this for at least six friends, and try to use two different adjectives each time. You could, of course, also write something about 'friends' whom you don't like!

Relationships 2

Basic grammar

CREDIT

Verb forms

When giving a more detailed account of relationships, you need to be able to describe what people **do** (or don't do) to make them good friends. In order to do this accurately, you need to be able to use verbs in the er / sie form, as well as in the wir form. Look at how you would describe one good friend in particular:

Er / sie **ist** ein guter Freund / eine gute Freundin.	He / she is a good friend.
Er / sie **versteht** mich.	He / she understands me.
Er / sie **hat** Respekt für mich.	He / she respects me.
Er / sie **geht** mir nie hinter den Rücken.	He / she never goes behind my back.
Er / sie **hat** einen Sinn für Humor.	He / she has a good sense of humour.
Er / sie **kann** ein Geheimnis behüten.	He / she can keep a secret.

… and how you would describe how you and others get along:

Meine Mutter und ich **haben** *eine enge Beziehung.*

My mother and I have a close relationship (we are close).

Mein bester Freund / meine beste Freundin / meine besten Freunde und ich **streiten** *nie.*

My best friend (male) / my best friend (female) / my best friends and I never argue.

Mein bester Freund / meine beste Freundin / meine besten Freunde und ich **sind** *einander sehr treu.*

My best friend (male) / my best friend (female) / my best friends and I are very loyal to each other.

The next examples show you ways to describe someone whom you don't particularly like:

Er / sie **ärgert** *mich.*
   He / she irritates me.

Er / sie **nervt** *mich.*
   He / she annoys me.

Er / sie **geht** *mir auf den Wecker.*
   He / she gets on my nerves.

Er / sie **hat** *eine Schraube locker.*
   He / she has a screw loose.

Er / sie **ist** *kindisch.*
   He / she is childish.

Er / sie **hat** *nicht alle Tassen im Schrank.*
   He / she is not all there.

Top Tip

If you are doing a Speaking assessment where you have to give opinions of others, make sure that you can use a variety of adjectives and phrases, and give reasons to back up what you have said. If you use a conjunction such as ' …, weil …' remember to send the verb in the next clause to the end, e.g. *Ich komme mit meinem Opa sehr gut aus,* **weil** *er einen guten Sinn für Humor* **hat**. (See the note on the following page on use of these conjunctions.)

Extended grammar

To further expand on **reasons** for good or poor relationships with others, you will have to use various conjunctions to connect your statements. As you have seen already, certain conjunctions change the word order of a sentence:

Subordinate clauses

A subordinate clause is part of a sentence.

Ich war glücklich, <u>als ich jung war.</u>   I was happy <u>when I was young</u>.

This part of the sentence is a subordinate clause.

A subordinate clause starts with a subordinating conjunction, e.g.

wenn	whenever, if	*wie*	how
weil	because	*bevor*	before
als	when (in the past)	*ehe*	before
da	since (because)	*nachdem*	after
ob	whether	*soweit*	as far (as ...)
obwohl	although	*sooft*	as often (as ...)
seit	since (a period of time)	*sobald*	as soon as
während	while	*dass*	that

If you start a sentence in German with one of these subordinating conjunctions, the verb must go to the end of that clause, e.g.

<u>Wenn</u> das Wetter gut <u>ist</u> ...   If the weather's good ...

subordinating   verb to end
   conjunction

The next clause must then start with a verb, e.g.

    1st clause   2nd clause

<u>Wenn</u> das Wetter gut <u>ist</u>,   <u>spiele</u> ich Tennis.   If the weather's good, I play tennis.

subordinating   verb–comma–verb
  conjunction

You must always apply the 'verb–comma–verb' rule whenever you start a sentence with any of these subordinating conjunctions.

If you use a subordinating conjunction in the middle of a sentence, then it sends the verb to the end of that clause only (i.e. it does not affect the previous word order) e.g.

normal word order   subordinate clause

Wir spielen heute Tennis,   weil das Wetter schön ist.

subordinating conjunction

We are playing tennis today because the weather is nice.

When you have a subordinate clause at the beginning of the sentence, you can still apply the 'verb–comma–verb' rule, even when you have more than one verb in the clause. This time you put the 'changing verb' from clause 1 to the end of that clause (before the comma) – like this:

clause 1

Da ich meine Hausaufgaben nicht gemacht habe, ...

past participle   'changing verb'

Because I've not done my homework ...

and clause 2's 'changing verb' now comes next:

clause 2

Da ich meine Hausaufgaben nicht gemacht habe, werde ich ...

'changing verb' comma 'changing verb'

Because I've not done my homework, I will ...

and the other verb(s) in clause 2 go to the end: clause 2

Da ich meine Hausaufgaben nicht gemacht habe, werde ich nicht ausgehen können.

past participle   'changing verb' comma 'changing verb' other verbs in clause 2

Because I've not done my homework, I will not be able to go out.

So the rule for sentences containing a subordinate clause is:
'changing verb–comma–changing verb'.

Perfect

Als wir in Deutschland <u>gewohnt</u> <u>haben</u>, <u>haben</u> wir oft Schwarzbrot <u>gegessen</u>.

                past participle   'changing verb' 'changing verb'   past participle

When we lived in Germany, we often ate rye bread.

Future

Wenn du deine Hausaufgaben nicht <u>machen</u> <u>wirst</u>, <u>wirst</u> du schlechte Noten <u>bekommen</u>.

             infinitive 'changing verb' 'changing verb'   infinitive

If you don't do your homework, you'll get poor grades.

Modal

Sobald ich meine Arbeit fertig <u>machen</u> <u>kann</u>, <u>komme</u> ich zur Party!

           infinitive   'changing verb'   'changing verb'

As soon as I can finish my work, I'm coming to the party!

Quick Test

Make up three other sentences like the ones above. Remember to ask your teacher to check them.

Relationships 3

Exercise 1

Sort these adjectives into two columns: POSITIVE and NEGATIVE.
(Turning the page is not allowed!)

ruhig	*geduldig*
lieb	*geizig*
egoistisch	*langweilig*
aufgeschlossen	*vernünftig*
verklemmt	*schüchtern*
ehrlich	*gemein*
sensibel	*großzügig*

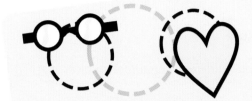

learning off by heart

Exercise 2

Read these letters written to an agony aunt, Tante Maria. Note down the
various problems, giving as much detail as possible.

Liebe Tante Maria …

*Ich schreibe dir im großen Notfall: ich habe Liebeskummer. Ich bin in einen Freund
meines älteren Bruders verliebt. Er ist neunzehn, groß, und hübsch. Er behandelt mich
wie eine Erwachsene, er hat viel Zeit für mich, aber er hat gar keine Ahnung,
dass ich diese Gefühle habe.*

*Ich bin erst vierzehn, aber ich weiß, dass es wahre Liebe ist. Ich habe
nicht gewagt, mit meinem Bruder darüber zu sprechen, weil er
mich auslachen würde. Ich komme mit meinem Bruder wirklich
sehr gut aus, aber so etwas zuzugeben wäre mir so peinlich!*

*Ich träume von ihm die ganze Zeit und kann mich nicht auf
meine Schularbeit richtig konzentrieren, ich habe dieses Jahr
kein gutes Zeugnis bekommen, weil die Schule für mich so
langweilig und schwierig geworden ist … ich möchte mit ihm
ausgehen … was soll ich tun?*

Katja

Liebe Tante Maria …

Ich schreibe dir, um deine Hilfe zu bitten. Ich habe ein großes Problem mit meiner 'neuen' Familie: ich bin Einzelkind und meine Eltern sind seit zwei Jahren geschieden, ich wohne mit meiner Mutter, aber ich sehe meinen Vater regelmäßig zweimal pro Monat. Das Problem ist – meine Mutter hat jetzt einen neuen Mann, der neulich bei uns eingezogen ist. Früher war es nur Mama und ich und wir hatten ein sehr gutes Verhältnis, aber jetzt muss ich meine Mama mit diesem Mann teilen, was ich nicht ausstehen kann. Er hat zwei Kinder, die am Wochenende zu uns kommen. Sie sind jünger als ich (acht und zehn) und ich muss mein Zimmer mit ihnen teilen, weil unsere Wohnung so klein ist, aber niemand hat mich gebeten, mein Zimmer zu teilen, es ist ja einfach ohne Besprechung vorgekommen. Noch schlimmer: ich kann die zwei Kinder nicht leiden; sie sind unordentlich, sie nehmen meine Klamotten, klauen meine CDs und wollen die ganze Zeit Kindersendungen anschauen. Es ist einfach ungerecht. Mit meinem 'Ersatzvater' habe ich auch große Schwierigkeiten: er behandelt mich wie ein Kind (ich bin fünfzehn) und ist streng; letzte Woche zum Beispiel, hat er es mir verboten, mit meinen Freunden ins Kino zu gehen, weil ich zu viele Hausaufgaben hatte.

Ich weiß nicht, was ich tun soll.

Michael

Top Tip

Try learning adjectives in pairs of opposites, e.g. *freundlich – unfreundlich.* Using your own knowledge, or your dictionary, write out the **opposites** of as many of the adjectives covered thus far as possible. And, as usual, learn any new vocabulary off by heart.

Quick Test   CREDIT

Imagine you are Tante Maria and write a few lines of advice to help solve Katja's and Michael's problems …! e.g.

Lieber Michael!

Zuerst musst du unbedingt mit deiner Mutter über dieses große Problem sprechen, damit sie Bescheid weiß, dass du so unglücklich bist …

Health issues 1

Basic vocabulary

Body parts

der Kopf	head
der Arm	arm
der Bauch	stomach / belly
der Fuß	foot
der Rücken	back
der Magen	stomach
der Ellbogen	elbow
der Mund	mouth
der Hals	throat
der Finger	finger
der Zeh	toe
die Nase	nose
die Hand	hand
die Schulter	shoulder
die Zunge	tongue
die Haut	skin
das Bein	leg
das Fußgelenk	ankle
das Handgelenk	wrist
das Herz	heart
das Knie	knee
das Auge	eye
das Ohr	ear

Ailments

der Stich	insect sting
der blaue Fleck	bruise
der Durchfall	diarrhoea
der Schmerz / die Schmerzen	pain(s)
der Fieber	fever / temperature
der Sonnenbrand	sunburn
die Krankheit	illness
die Reisekrankheit	travel sickness
die Seekrankheit	sea sickness
die Erkältung	cold (the illness)
die Schwellung	swelling
die Grippe	flu
die Magenverstimmung	indigestion
die Brandwunde	burn
die Verstopfung	constipation
die Verletzung	injury
die Schnittwunde	cut
die Lebensmittelvergiftung	food poisoning

Top Tip
If you need to buy medicines or collect a prescription in Germany, you'll have to find *eine Apotheke*. This is different from *eine Drogerie*, where you can buy toiletries, but not medicines.

Top Tip
When you are asking the chemist for medicines in German, you have to ask '*Haben Sie etwas **gegen** …?*' – *gegen* means 'against', so you are asking for something to **combat** illness, not something **for** illness, as we say in English, which could mean something to **give** you an illness!

Extended vocabulary

The dispensing chemist's

die Apotheke	chemist's (dispenses medicines)
die Tablette	tablet
der Saft	liquid medicine
der Pflaster	plaster
Medikamente	medicines
das Rezept	prescription
Hustenbonbons	cough sweets
die Pille	pill
der Verband	bandage
Tropfen	drops
eine Salbe	ointment
die Schlinge	sling

Doctor's, hospital and dentist's

der Unfall	accident
der Krankenwagen	ambulance
das Krankenhaus	hospital
die Krankenkasse	medical insurance
der Notfall	emergency
der Krankenschein	doctor's note, exempting you from work
die Sprechstunde	surgery hours
der Arzt	doctor
der Zahnarzt	dentist
die Krankenschwester	nurse (female)
der Krankenpfleger	nurse (male)
die Operation	operation
die Spritze	injection
der Wartesaal	waiting room
die Füllung / die Plombe	filling

The drugstore

die Zahnbürste	toothbrush
die Zahnpasta	toothpaste
die Haarbürste	hairbrush
die Watte	cotton wool
die Seife	soap
der Rasierapparat	razor
das Shampoo	shampoo

Quick Test

Once you have learned the vocabulary properly, cover up the list, then label this picture of a *dispensing* chemist's shop.

Health issues 2

Basic grammar

Saying what's wrong

To be able to explain what is wrong with you, make sure you understand a variety of questions about your health:

Wo tut es (dir) weh?	Where is it sore?
Was ist los (mit dir)?	What is wrong (with you)?
Was hast du?	What's wrong?

Top Tip

When you are talking about allergies, once again, you use the German word for 'against', e.g. '... *ich bin allergisch gegen Meeresfrüchte und Waschpulver ... und Hausarbeit!*

Singular:

For masculine and neuter nouns, use **mein** + part of the body; for feminine nouns, use **meine** + part of the body.

e.g.

*Mein Arm **tut** weh.*

*Mein Bein **tut** weh.*

*Meine Nase **tut** weh.*

Plural:

For all genders in the plural, when you are stating what is wrong, use **meine** + body parts and change *tut weh* to **tun weh.**

e.g.

*Meine Augen **tun** weh.*

*Meine Finger **tun** weh.*

*Meine Hände **tun** weh.*

You can also talk about certain aches and pains by adding **-schmerzen** to the word for certain body parts.

e.g.

Ich habe Halsschmerzen.

Ich habe Zahnschmerzen.

Ich habe Magenschmerzen.

Ich habe Rückenschmerzen.

Top Tip

If you are doing a role-play Speaking assessment on illnesses, always have a few extra ailments at your disposal which you can add to the dialogue with your teacher; that way you can hopefully extend the conversation, and try to 'take control' of the assessment on your own terms, to help improve your grade!

Quick Test

Translate the ten ailments above into English (without turning the page!).

When you are talking about other people's ailments, you need to be able to use the correct form of the verb *haben* with *er* and *sie* as well as knowing how to say 'his' and 'her' – look over your own grammar notes on this point and use the notes below as vocabulary practice and revision!

Er / sie **hat** *eine Grippe.*

He / she has the flu.

Er / sie **hat** *Ohrenschmerzen.*

He / she has earache.

Er / sie **hat** *Durchfall.*

He / she has diarrhoea.

Singular form – males:

(m) sein *Fuß tut weh*	**his** foot is sore
(nt) sein *Ohr tut weh*	**his** ear is sore
(f) seine *Schulter tut weh*	**his** shoulder is sore

Singular form – females:

(m) ihr *Kopf tut weh*	**her** head is sore
(nt) ihr *Auge tut weh*	**her** eye is sore
(f) ihre *Zunge tut weh*	**her** tongue is sore

Plural:

seine *Beine tun weh*	**his** legs are sore
seine *Arme tun weh*	**his** arms are sore
seine *Zehe tun weh*	**his** toes are sore

Plural:

ihre *Füße tun weh*	**her** feet are sore
ihre *Augen tun weh*	**her** eyes are sore
ihre *Ohren tun weh*	**her** ears are sore

Extended grammar

CREDIT

The perfect tense

To explain in more detail about what happened to make you ill or how you were injured, you will have to use the Perfect Tense (see page 98 of the Grammar section).

Ich **habe** *mir in den Finger* **geschnitten.**	I've cut my finger.
Eine Wespe **hat** *mir in den Arm* **gestochen.**	A wasp has stung me on the arm.
Er **hat** *zu viel Bier* **getrunken.**	He has drunk too much beer.
Sie **hat** *zu viel Kuchen* **gegessen.**	She has eaten too much cake.
Er **hat** *sich das Fußgelenk* **verrenkt.**	He has twisted his ankle.
Sie **hat** *sich das Handgelenk* **verstaucht.**	She has sprained her wrist.
Ich **habe** *einen Sonnenbrand* **bekommen.**	I've got sunburn.

Quick Test

Tut or **tun** weh?

(Do this test very quickly, **without** looking at the previous page!)

1 *Meine Augen …*

2 *Seine Nase …*

3 *Ihre Hand …*

4 *Mein Bein …*

5 *Ihre Schulter …*

6 *Seine Füße …*

7 *Meine Ohren …*

8 *Ihr Rücken …*

Health issues 3

Exercise 1

Match up the various ailments with the pictures.

a. *Meine Schulter tut weh.*

b. *Ich bin seekrank.*

c. *Ich habe Fieber.*

d. *Ich habe eine Schnittwunde.*

e. *Ich bin erkältet.*

f. *Ich habe Halsschmerzen.*

  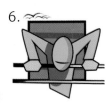

Exercise 2

Now look at the list below. Find the labels of the body parts and copy them into the correct place on the picture. Then find the ailments and draw an arrow from each ailment to the correct place on the picture.

der Fuß

mein Auge tut weh

ich habe eine Lebensmittelvergiftung

das Herz

ich habe Rückenschmerzen

die Nase

das Handgelenk

ich habe Ohrenschmerzen

mein Ellbogen tut weh

der Arm

ich habe mir das Fußgelenk verrenkt

die Schulter

meine Zehe tun weh

Exercise 3

Listen to and read through this dialogue set in a chemist's, then answer the questions in English.

CHEMIST   *Guten Morgen, kann ich Ihnen helfen?*

TOURIST   *Guten Morgen, ja … ich bin hier mit meiner Familie im Urlaub und wir sind alle ein bisschen krank …*

CHEMIST   *Ja, was ist denn mit Ihnen los?*

TOURIST *Nun, sehen Sie, es ist ein wenig peinlich. Wir wohnen in der 'Pension Rosenkranz' hier gegenüber und ... das Problem ist, wir sind alle allergisch gegen das Frühstück, das wir jeden Morgen bekommen! Marmelade, Schwarzbrot und Eier, so typisch Deutsch, wir können es einfach nicht länger aushalten! Es ist ekelhaft! Ich habe jeden Tag Durchfall, meine Frau leidet an Verstopfung und mein Sohn hat einen Hautausschlag! Es ist ja furchtbar, und wir wagen es einfach nicht, das Frühstück stehen zu lassen, weil die Wirtin so böse ist! Sie ist eine Hexe! Bitte, können Sie uns etwas empfehlen?!*

CHEMIST *Ja, natürlich empfehle ich ihnen etwas – diese Tabletten hier tun gut. Morgen früh nimmt die ganze Familie 10 Tabletten nach dem Frühstück mit einem Liter Wasser dazu und dann joggen Sie drei Kilometer zum nächsten Dorf, wo Sie eine andere Pension finden können. Damit Sie Bescheid wissen: die 'Pension Rosenkranz' gehört meiner Familie. Mein achtzigjähriger Vater steht jeden Morgen um 4 Uhr auf, um das Schwarzbrot zu backen, meine neunundsiebzigjährige Mutter kocht jeden Nachmittag die Marmelade und die Eier sind vom Bauernhof meines lieblingonkels. Adieu!*

1 What health problems has the family had during their stay?
2 What has caused this?
3 How does the tourist manage to further offend the chemist?
4 What remedy and advice does the chemist give him?
5 What information does the chemist give about the breakfast?!

Quick Test

Below is a list of vocabulary from the dialogue. Fill in the English, either from your own knowledge, or by looking up the dictionary.

GERMAN	ENGLISH
ein wenig	
peinlich	
Eier	
leiden	
Hautausschlag	
wagen	
ablegen	
die Wirtin	
böse	
empfehlen	
damit	
Bescheid wissen	
beliebt	
Adieu	

... and now learn these words off by heart!

Environment 1

Basic vocabulary

Nature

In general, German society is very environmentally aware, and has been so for a long time. As a result, it is a topic which crops up in exams.

die Bäume	trees
die Natur	nature
die Insekten	insects
die Tiere	animals
die Pflanzen	plants
gefährdete Tier- und Pflanzarten	
	endangered animals and plants
die Blumen	flowers
die Felder	fields
die Flüsse	rivers
die Wälder	forests
die Wiesen	meadows
das Tal	valley
die Vögel	birds
die Fische	fish
die Erde	earth
die Landschaft	landscape
das Naturschutzgebiet	nature reserve

Environmental issues

die Atmosphäre	atmosphere
die Luft	air
die Autos	cars
die Abfälle	litter
der Lärm	noise
die Verpackungen (pl.)	packaging
die Umwelt	the environment
die Verschwendung	waste
der Verkehr	traffic
schaden	to damage
schonen	to conserve
vermeiden	to avoid
das Recycling	recycling
die Vorteile	advantages
die Nachteile	disadvantages

Top Tip

Write the word *Umwelt* (environment) in a circle in the middle of a blank sheet of paper. Then make a 'spidergraph' of as many words as possible that you associate with this topic, from memory. If you get stuck, refer back to this page.

Extended vocabulary

das Abwasser	sewage
das Altglas	recycled glass
das Altpapier	recycled paper
das Alu	tin foil
die Atomenergie	atomic energy
das Atomkraftwerk	nuclear power station
die Autoabgase	exhaust fumes
die Dosen	cans
Energie sparen	to save energy
die Fabrik	factory
die Flaschen	bottles
die Folgen	consequences
die Einwegflaschen	non-returnable bottles
die Mehrwegflaschen	returnable bottles
die Pfandflaschen	returnable bottles
das Gas	gas
die Grünen	the Green Party
das Hauptproblem	main problem
die Klimaveränderung	climate change
die Kohle	coal
die Lösung	solution
die Luftverschmutzung	air pollution
der Meeresspiegel	sea-level
der Müll	rubbish
die öffentlichen Verkehrsmittel	public transport
die Ökologie	ecology
das Öko-System	eco-system
das Öl	oil
der Öltanker	oil tanker
der Ölteppich	oil slick
das Ozonloch	hole in the ozone
die Plasiktüte	plastic bag
der Qualm	smoke
den Regenwald vernichten	to destroy the rain-forest
der Recyclingcontainer	recycling container
die Tankerkatastrophe	tanker accident
der Treibhauseffekt	greenhouse effect
umweltfreundliche Produkte	environmentally friendly products
der Umweltschutz	environmental protection
die Umweltverschmutzung	pollution
umweltfreundlich	environmentally friendly
umweltfeindlich	environmentally damaging
der Unfall	accident
die Waldrodung	deforestation
die Wasservorräte (pl.)	water reserves
die Wasserverseuchung	water contamination
die Windenergie	wind power

Exercise 1

Choose 15 of the above issues, and write them in German in your order of importance for the environment. Now ask a friend to give you their top 15 issues from the list. Write them down in German, and compare the two lists to find out how many things you agree on.

Quick Test

Look at these parts of words from the above list. Find and write down the complete words, with their English meanings:

1 veränderung   (die)

2 abgase   (die)

3 spiegel   (der)

4 verschmutzung   (die)

5 glas   (das)

6 tüte   (die)

Environment 2

Basic grammar

Inversion

If you have to discuss, read or write about environmental issues, it is useful to have some good 'starter phrases' to help you understand and express opinions:

In erster Linie …	In the first place …
Zweitens …	Secondly …
Meiner Meinung nach …	In my opinion …
Auf der einen Seite …	On the one hand …
Auf der anderen Seite …	On the other hand …
Ehrlich gesagt …	To be honest …
In der Regel …	As a rule …
In Wirklichkeit …	In reality …
Zum Schluss …	In conclusion …

CREDIT

Following on from these starter phrases comes the point that is being made. This means that inversion must be used – i.e. the verb appears next in the sentence.

Some examples of how this works:

In erster Linie verschwenden wir zu viel Energie. = In the first place, we waste too much energy.

Zweitens verseuchen wir die Nordsee. = Secondly, we are contaminating the North Sea.

Meiner Meinung nach ist es wichtig, Altpapier zu benutzen.

= In my opinion, it is important to use recycled paper.

Auf der einen Seite roden sie den Wald immer schneller.

= On the one hand, they are clearing the forests faster and faster.

Auf der anderen Seite vernichten sie den Regenwald.

= On the other hand, they are destroying the rain-forest.

Ehrlich gesagt finde ich Atomenergie äußerst gefährlich.

= To be honest, I find nuclear energy extremely dangerous.

In Wirklichkeit nehmen viele Kunden die kostenlosen Plastiktüten.

= In reality, lots of customers take the free plastic bags.

In der Regel **trenne** *ich den Haushaltsmüll.* = As a rule, I **separate** the household rubbish.

Zum Schluss **muss** *man versuchen, umweltfreundlicher zu sein.*

= In conclusion, one **must** try to be more environmentally friendly.

Extended grammar

CREDIT

The conditional

In order to develop the points being made about the environment, you might want to suggest what possibilities there are to improve the situation. This involves the use of the **conditional**. We use it to say what **should / ought to**, **could** or **would have to** happen.

What **should** be done?

Man sollte global denken.	One / we ought to think globally.
Wir sollten dringend eine Lösung suchen.	We should look for a solution urgently.
*Wir **sollten** die Wälder retten.*	We **should** save the forests.

What **could** be done?

Man könnte Autoabgase reduzieren.	One / we could reduce car exhaust fumes.
Man könnte umweltfreundliche Produkte kaufen.	One / we could buy environmentally friendly products.
*Wir **könnten** gefährdete Tierarten schützen.*	We **could** protect endangered species.

What **would have** to be done?

*Wir **müssten** mehr Wasser sparen.*	We **would have to** save more water.
Man müsste Windenergie benutzen.	One / we would have to use wind energy.
Man müsste den Haushaltsmüll getrennt sammeln.	One / we would have to gather the household rubbish as separate items.

Top Tip

Expressions like these can be very useful for Credit Writing Folio pieces. You do not need to use many of them, but a few included in your concluding paragraph will demonstrate that you are able to express yourself on a more sophisticated level.

Quick Test

Translate the following sentences into English:

1 *Ehrlich gesagt ist das Hauptproblem die Energieverschwendung.*

2 *Wir sollten mit öffentlichen Verkehrsmitteln fahren.*

3 *Man müsste es in der Schule lernen.*

Quick Test

You are taking part in a debate on the environment. Prepare your notes, outlining the main problems and issues. Remember to use the 'starter phrases' to emphasise your points.

Environment 3

Exercise 1

Listen to and read the comments on the environment which these three politicians are making.

Read the statements in English below and identify the speakers for each.

Frau Grünewald

In der Regel verschwenden wir viel zu viel Wasser. Man sollte die Wasservorräte sparen. Viele große Fabriken verseuchen auch das Wasser mit Chemikalien, was ich äußerst schlimm finde. Das gefährdet das Öko-System, nicht nur in Deutschland, sondern auf der ganzen Welt.

Herr Steinherz

Meiner Meinung nach ist die Klimaveränderung ein großes Problem, aber auf der anderen Seite könnten wir neue Atomkraftwerke bauen. Dabei vermeiden wir die Luftverschmutzung und zur gleichen Zeit schonen wir die Landschaft. In Wirklichkeit könnten wir einfach nicht genug Windenergie produzieren.

Frau Rosenthal

In erster Linie finde ich, dass man sehr oft mit dem Auto fährt, was der Umwelt sehr schadet. Kein Wunder, dass die Luftverschmutzung ein großes Problem für uns ist. Deshalb sollte man öfters die fantastischen öffentlichen Verkehrsmittel benutzen, damit könnte man die Autoabgase stark reduzieren.

1 We could build nuclear power stations. _____

2 We waste too much water. _____

3 Car travel damages the environment. _____

4 The eco-system is being destroyed, not only in Germany, but all over the world. _____

5 Realistically, we cannot produce enough wind energy. _____

6 A lot of big factories pollute the water. _____

Top Tip
As with all Listening tasks, check first what it is that you have to find out. In this exercise, for example, you know that the issues involved are country life versus city life. So while thinking about and listening for key words, you will also be listening for indicato[r] which give a hint about the direction the speaker is taking, e.g.:
zum Glück – fortunately
die Vorteile sind … – the advantages are …
die Nachteile sind … – the disadvantages are …
auf der anderen Seite – on the other hand

Exercise 2

Listen to and read through these arguments for and against life in the country and town. For each person, give details of the pros and cons.

Ich kann mir nicht vorstellen, irgendwo anders als hier in der Stadtmitte Berlins zu wohnen. Hier habe ich mein ganzes Leben gelebt. Was ich gut daran finde, ist dass man kein Auto braucht, weil die Verkehrsverbindungen so toll sind – besonders die U-Bahn und die S-Bahn. Jeden Tag komme ich mit der U-Bahn ins Büro. Die Vorteile sind: es ist viel billiger als ein Auto zu kaufen, es ist schnell und zuverlässig und schont wir die Umwelt.

Gibt es überhaupt Nachteile? Na ja, manchmal möchte ich nach der Arbeit einen schönen Spaziergang machen, aber dafür müsste ich wieder mit der U-Bahn fahren, um zu den Grünanlagen zu kommen. Natürlich kann man auch nicht am Strand spazieren gehen, weil Berlin so weit von der Küste liegt.

Klaus, 31 Jahre

Ich wohne auf einem Bauernhof, wo man Bio-Lebensmittel produziert.

Auf der einen Seite ist das Leben auf dem Lande sehr ruhig und angenehm, weil es nicht zu viel Lärm gibt, oder die Hektik, die man in der Stadt findet. Weil diese Gegend ein Naturschutzgebiet ist, sind die Flüsse unverseucht und die Luft bleibt unverschmutzt. Man schont auch die gefährdeten Tier- und Pflanzarten, die man in den Wäldern und Wiesen finden kann. Zum Glück hat man hier keinen Wald gerodet, um neue Wohnsiedlungen zu bauen.

Auf der anderen Seite gibt es für Jugendliche auf dem Lande nicht viel zu tun, besonders wenn man auf einem Bauernhof wohnt. Leider gibt es kein Nachtleben, weil die Busverbindungen sehr schlecht sind, und der letzte Bus von der nächsten Stadt schon um halb zehn fährt.

Trude, 14 Jahre

	Town Pros	Town Cons	Country Pros	Country Cons
Klaus				
Trude				

Quick Test

Find the German in the above texts for:

1 ... and at the same time, we are protecting the environment.
2 Unfortunately, there's no night life.
3 I live on a farm where organic food is produced.
4 Are there any disadvantages at all?
5 I can't imagine living anywhere other than here in the middle of Berlin.

One World

Basic vocabulary

Countries and continents

Europa	Europe
Afrika	Africa
Nordamerika	North America
Südamerika	South America
Asien	Asia
Australien	Australia

German speaking countries

die Bundesrepublik Deutschland	
	the Federal Republic of Germany
Österreich	Austria
die Schweiz	Switzerland

European countries

Großbritannien	Great Britain
Schottland	Scotland
England	England
Wales	Wales
Nordirland	Northern Ireland
Irland	Ireland
Frankreich	France
Dänemark	Denmark
Italien	Italy
die Niederlande	the Netherlands
Belgien	Belgium
Luxemburg	Luxembourg
Norwegen	Norway
Schweden	Sweden
Spanien	Spain
Portugal	Portugal
Griechenland	Greece
Polen	Poland
Ungarn	Hungary
die Tschechische Republik	Czech Republic
Slowakei	Slovakia
Estland	Estonia
Lettland	Latvia
Litauen	Lithuania
Kroatien	Croatia
die Türkei	Turkey

People

die Briten	the British
die Schotten	the Scots
die Engländer	the English
die Iren	the Irish
die Waliser	the Welsh
die Deutschen	the Germans
die Franzosen	the French
die Italiener	the Italians
die Spanier	the Spanish
die Holländer	the Dutch
die Griechen	the Greeks
die Portugiesen	the Portugese
die Belgier	the Belgians
die Polen	the Poles
die Schweizer	the Swiss

Religions, etc.

die Christen	Christians
die Katholiker	Catholics
die Protestanten	Protestants
die Juden	Jews
die Moslemen	Muslims
die Moschee	mosque
die Hindus	Hindus
die Sikhen	Sikhs
die Einwanderer	immigrants
die Asylbewerber	asylum seekers
die Gastarbeiter	guest (immigrant) workers
sprechen	speak ...
deutsch	German
türkisch	Turkish
polnisch	Polish

Top Tip
To give a **nationality**, a capital letter is used: *Er ist **Deutsche***. To give the **language** spoken, a small letter is used: *Er spricht **deutsch***.

Extended vocabulary

CREDIT

Geography

die See / das Meer	sea
der See	lake
die Nordsee	North Sea
die Ostsee	Baltic Sea
das Mittelmeer	Mediterranean
der Bodensee	Lake Constance
der Atlantische Ozean	Atlantic Ocean
die Pazifik	the Pacific
die Donau	the Danube
der Rhein	the Rhine
Genf	Geneva
Venedig	Venice
Wien	Vienna
die Alpen	the Alps
die Hauptstadt	capital
die Einwohner	inhabitants / natives
die Erde	earth
das Klima	climate
die Naturkatastrophe	natural disaster
die Wüste	desert
der Fluß	river
die Dürre	drought
die Überflutung	flooding
das Erdbeben	earthquake

Lifestyle issues

Aids	Aids
die Armut	poverty
die dritte Welt	the third world
die Liebe	love
die Einstellung	attitude
die Ernährung	diet, food
die Kenntnisse (pl.)	knowledge
der Glaube	faith
kulturelle Unterschiede	cultural differences
Glaubensunterschiede	religious differences
die Essgewohnheiten	eating habits
die Geburt	birth
die Schule	school
das Schulsystem	school system
die Bildung	education
die Kinder	children
der Hass	hatred

die Heimat	country of origin
der Fremdenhass	hatred of foreigners
die Scham	shame
die Sterbeziffer	mortality rate
der Tod	death
die (Mutter)sprache	(native) language
die Lebensweise	way of life
die Moralität	morality
die Staatsangehörigkeit	nationality
der Rassismus	racism
die Regenzeit	rainy season
der Respekt	respect
der Reichtum	wealth
die Unwissenheit	ignorance

Quick Test

Put into English:

1 Viele Belgier sprechen französisch.

2 Die Asylbewerber sind aus aller Welt gekommen.

3 Viele Gastarbeiter sind Türken.

4 Viele Einwanderer kommen nach Deutschland.

Quick Test

Find the opposite of these words:

1 die Dürre

2 der Tod

3 die Kenntnisse

4 die Liebe

5 die Einwohner

6 die Armut

One World 2

Basic grammar

Germany, like some other European countries, has a number of large immigrant communities, one of which is Turkish. This goes back to the 1950s and 1960s, when many Turkish men came to work in the construction industry in Germany during the 'Economic Miracle'. They were known as **Gastarbeiter** (guest workers).

Eventually, many of them brought their families over to settle in Germany, and nowadays there are over 5 million people of Turkish extraction, many of them second and third generation Germans. This section will include vocabulary relevant to some of their experiences and situations.

Since the 1990s, many people from the Eastern block countries have also settled in Germany. So now, there is a word that is used frequently – **multikulti**!

Verbs ending in **-en**

arbeiten	to work
Asyl erhalten	to be granted asylum
bringen	to bring
folgen	to follow
sprechen	to speak
suchen	to look for
verdienen	to earn
verlassen	to leave
zahlen	to pay

Top Tip
Note how **man** is used here as a way of saying **they / people**. It is also used to mean **'you'** do or **'one'** does something. It is very common to use this form in German, and is not at all 'posh' to use it!

Some phrases using **-en** verbs:

Man arbeitet / sie arbeiten auf Baustellen.	People / they work on building sites.
Man bringt / sie bringen die eigene Kultur.	People / they bring their own culture.
Man erhält / sie erhalten Asyl.	People / they are granted asylum.
Man folgt / sie folgen den Männern nach Deutschland.	People / they follow the men to Germany.
Man spricht / sie sprechen die Muttersprache.	People / they speak their native language.
Man sucht / sie suchen Arbeit.	People / they look for work.
Man lernt / sie lernen deutsch.	People / they learn German.
Man verdient / sie verdienen nicht viel.	People / they don't earn much.
Man verlässt / sie verlassen die Heimat.	People / they leave their homes.
Man zahlt / sie zahlen eine hohe Miete.	People / they pay a high rent.

Extended grammar

Here are three more types of verbs you can use in this context:

Separable verbs

auswandern	to emigrate	*einwandern*	to immigrate

Man wandert / sie wandern von der Heimat aus.   People / they emigrate from their native country.

Man wandert / sie wandern in ein neues Land ein.   People / they emigrate to a new country.

Verbs ending in *-ieren*

integrieren	to integrate	*akzeptieren*	to accept

Man integriert / sie integrieren die Kinder in die Schulen.

People / they integrate the children into the schools.

Man akzeptiert / sie akzeptiern sie nicht immer.   People / they don't always accept them.

Reflexive verbs

sich um Asyl bewerben	to apply for asylum	*sich einleben*	to settle down
sich kennenlernen	to get to know	*sich verstehen mit*	to get along with
sich bemühen	to try hard		

Man bewirbt sich um Asyl.   People / they apply for asylum.

Man lebt sich langsam ein.   People / they settle down slowly.

Man lernt sich kennen.   People / they get to know each other.

Man versteht sich mit den Nachbarn.   People / they get along with the neighbours.

Man bemüht sich, die neuen Sitten zu lernen.   People / they try hard to learn the new customs.

Quick Test

Put the following sentences into a logical sequence:

1 *Man lebt sich langsam ein.*

2 *Die Männer verlassen die Heimat.*

3 *Man bemüht sich, die neuen Sitten zu lernen.*

4 *Man spricht nur die Muttersprache.*

5 *Die Familien folgen den Männern.*

6 *Sie wandern in ein neues Land ein.*

7 *Sie arbeiten auf Baustellen.*

8 *Man versteht sich gut mit den Nachbarn.*

9 *Sie suchen Arbeit.*

10 *Man bringt die eigene Kultur mit.*

11 *Sie lernen deutsch.*

One World 3

Exercise 1

15 ◯

CREDIT

Listen to and read this interview with Mehmet, who is a German boy of Turkish descent.

Draw two columns, one with the heading *Türkisch* and the other *Deutsch*. Into each column, put key words which indicate each aspect of Mehmet's life.

Interviewer:
> Also Mehmet, wie lange wohnst du schon in Deutschland?

Mehmet:
> Eigentlich bin ich hier vor fünfzehn Jahren geboren.

I Tatsächlich? Und wo bist du geboren?

M In Dortmund. Damals hat meine Familie dort gewohnt.

I Und deine Eltern? Sind sie auch in Dortmund geboren?

M Ja, aber meine Großeltern sind 1967 aus der Türkei ausgewandert, und haben sich hier eingelebt.

I Und konnten sie deutsch sprechen?

M Kein Wort! Mein Opa hat auf einer Baustelle gearbeitet. Meine Großeltern sprechen immer noch kein gutes deutsch.

I Und deine Eltern? Sprechen sie deutsch?

M Ja, klar! Mein Vater hat eine gute Stelle bei Audi, im Büro. Und meine Mutter ist Deutsche.

I Und was ist deine Muttersprache?

M Eigentlich deutsch – obwohl ich auch türkisch spreche, und wir sprechen oft türkisch zu Hause.

I Und wie ist es mit den Essgewohnheiten bei dir? Esst ihr immer typisches türkisches Essen?

M Nicht immer, aber zu Bairan essen wir türkisch. Das ist ein türkisches Fest. Mein Vater und ich gehen in die Moschee. Dann kommen wir nach Hause, wo meine Mutter ein großes Frühstück vorbereitet hat. Das ist ein großes Essen mit vielen türkischen Spezialitäten. Wir freuen uns immer darauf!

I Gehst du oft mit Freunden aus, Mehmet?

M Klar! Zwei- bis dreimal pro Woche gehen wir aus – zum Fußballtraining, in den Jugendklub oder ins Kino. Wir gehen besonders gern zu McDonalds, wo mein Lieblingsessen ein Big Mac ist.

I Sind deine Freunde alle aus türkischen Familien?

M Gar nicht! Ich habe allerlei Freunde – aus türkischen Familien, Deutsche, Russen, Inder, sogar aus Schottland!

I Hast du immer noch Verwandte in der Türkei?

M Oh ja! Ich habe jede Menge Tanten, Onkeln, Cousins und Cousinen dort. Wir sehen uns alle zwei Jahre, wenn wir da auf Urlaub sind. Aber am liebsten fahre ich im Winter nach Österreich, zum Skifahren.

Quick Test

Without referring to the vocabulary lists, find the German in the above transcript for:

1 I have loads of aunts and uncles.
2 We always look forward to it.
3 My father has a good job.
4 Do you still have relatives in Turkey?
5 All kinds of friends.

Exercise 2

 16

Read through and listen to this account of a family trip to Germany.

Vor zwei Jahren bin ich mit meiner Familie nach Hamburg gefahren. Zu der Zeit wohnten Freunde von meinen Eltern in einem Vorort, weil sie da an der Universität arbeiteten.

Da sie nur eine kleine Wohnung hatten, haben wir in einer kleinen Pension gewohnt, ganz in der Nähe der Uni. Jeden Tag, gleich nach dem Frühstück, machten wir einen kleinen Ausflug in die Stadt. Am ersten Tag haben wir den Fernsehturm besichtigt, um einen tollen Blick auf die Stadt zu haben. Aber noch besser waren die fantastischen Torten, die man da oben im Restaurant servierte!

Für €15 konnte man mit dem Aufzug nach oben fahren, und dann so viel Kuchen essen und Kaffee trinken wie man wollte!

Abends war es schön, einen Spaziergang in dem großen Park 'Planten un Blomen' zu machen.

Hamburg ist eine große Hafenstadt. Jeden Tag kommen Waren aus aller Welt in Containerschiffen hierher. Wir haben eine Hafenrundfahrt gemacht, und haben die Speicherstadt gesehen. Das waren alte Warenhäuser, randvoll mit Teppichen aus Indien, Möbeln, Kaffee, Getreide und viel em mehr.

Sonntagvormittag gingen wir zum Fischmarkt, wo man nicht nur Fisch kaufte, sondern Obst, Gemüse, Blumen, Kanarienvögel und Kaninchen – alles!

Ich habe viele schöne Erinnerungen an Hamburg, und möchte noch einmal diese faszinierende Stadt besuchen.

Now read this text again, and look out for which tenses are being used.

Remember, the Perfect Tense is used for completed actions or events, and the Imperfect Tense is used for descriptions and continuous actions in the past.

(See Tenses, pages 97–102.)

Top Tip
To use time phrases when you did something on a regular basis, you can add an 's' and use a small letter to start the word:
abends – in the evenings
sonntagvormittags: – on Sunday mornings
dienstags: – on Tuesdays

Quick Test

Find the German for these phrases:

Perfect Tense:

1 We took a trip round the harbour.

2 We stayed in a small bed & breakfast.

3 We visited the television tower.

4 I went to Hamburg with my family.

Quick Test

Find the German for these phrases:

Imperfect Tense:

1 We used to go to the fish market.

2 ... because they were working at the university.

3 Even better were the fantastic gateaux.

4 For €15 you could take the lift to the top.

5 Those were old warehouses.

6 At that time, friends lived ...

Cases and articles

Grammar is the study of how words are put together to make sentences. Learning grammar helps you understand what you read and hear. It also helps you speak well and write accurately.

Nouns and their cases

A noun is the name of a person or thing, e.g. 'dog', 'Elizabeth', 'desk', 'warmth'. All nouns in German are masculine, feminine or neuter. This is called their gender. They all start with a capital letter.

German nouns have four cases:
* nominative
* accusative
* genitive
* dative.

The nominative case

Nouns are listed in your German dictionary in the nominative case, so that you can find out if they are:
* masculine (m.) *'der'*
* feminine (f.) *'die'* or
* neuter (nt.) *'das'*.

'Der', *'die'* and *'das'* all mean 'the'; *'ein'* and *'eine'* mean 'a'.

The nominative case is the subject case. The subject of a sentence is the person or thing doing something, e.g.
Die Krankenschwester arbeitet nachts.
The nurse works nights.

Or the subject of a sentence is something, e.g.
Der Hund ist groß.
The dog is big.

The accusative case

The accusative case is used:

* for the direct object (the person or thing having something done to them), e.g.
Klaus trinkt den Kaffee.
Klaus drinks the coffee.

* with prepositions which take the accusative case, e.g.
Der Zug fährt durch einen Tunnel.
The train goes through a tunnel.

* with prepositions which take the accusative case when there is movement from one place to another, e.g.
Das Auto fährt über die Brücke.
The car goes over the bridge.

* in definite time phrases, e.g.
letzten Montag   last Monday.
den ganzen Abend   the whole evening.

The genitive case

The genitive case indicates possession or ownership, e.g.
der Deckel der Teekanne.
the lid of the teapot.

Das ist das Rad meines Freundes.
That is my friend's bike. (Literally 'That is the bike of my friend.')

The genitive case is also used with some prepositions, including:

trotz   in spite of
außerhalb   outside of
wegen   because of
während   during
innerhalb   inside of
(an)statt   instead of

The dative case

The dative case is used:

- to indicate 'to' or 'for', e.g.
  Ich habe meinem Onkel ein Geburtstagsgeschenk gegeben.
  I gave a birthday present to my uncle.

  Gibst du mir ein Bonbon?
  Can you give a sweet to me?

When the dative case is used like this, words such as '*meinem Onkel*' and '*mir*' are called the indirect object of the sentence.

- after prepositions which always take the dative case, e.g.
  Claudia geht mit dem Hund spazieren.
  Claudia goes for a walk with the dog.

- after prepositions which take the dative case when there is no movement from one place to another, e.g.
  Die Mikrowelle ist in der Küche.
  The microwave is in the kitchen.

The dative case is also used:

- after certain verbs, including *helfen* (to help), *danken* (to thank), *folgen* (to follow), *glauben* (to believe), *gehören* (to belong), *gelingen* (to succeed / manage), *wünschen* (to wish), e.g.

Kannst du mir helfen?	Can you help me?
Ich danke Ihnen.	Thank you.
Folgen Sie dem Taxi!	Follow that cab!

  Glaubst du dem Lehrer nicht?
  Don't you believe the teacher?

  Das gehört meiner Schwester.
  That belongs to my sister.

  Es gelingt dem Fußballspieler nicht, ein Tor zu schießen.
  The footballer can't manage to score a goal.

  Wir wünschen dir viel Glück!
  We wish you lots of luck.

The definite article 'the'

Case	Masculine	Feminine	Neuter	Plural
Nominative	der	die	das	die
Accusative	den	die	das	die
Genitive	des	der	des	der
Dative	dem	der	dem	den

The indefinite article 'a'

Masculine	Feminine	Neuter	Plural
ein	eine	ein	keine
einen	eine	ein	keine
eines	einer	eines	keiner
einem	einer	einem	keinen

dieser (this), *mancher* (some), *solcher* (such), *jener* (that), *welcher*? (which?) also have these endings.

There is no plural of *ein*. However, the adjective *kein* (no) and possessive adjectives (e.g. *mein* – my, *dein* – your) have these endings.

Quick Test

Choose the correct article to complete these sentences:

[Sein : Seine : Seinen] Schwester ist sehr hübsch.

Folgen Sie [der Mann : den Mann : dem Mann].

Er ist Manager [einer : eines : einem] Firma (f.) in Köln.

Prepositions and pronouns

Prepositions

• with • under • from • in • at • after

A preposition is a word used in combination with a noun to form a phrase, e.g.

> I go to the cinema with my friends.
>
> Did you get a letter from him?
>
> After the match, we got the bus home.

In German, there are three main categories of prepositions:

Category 1		Category 2		Category 3	
durch	through	*an*	to, at, on	*mit*	with
gegen	towards, about	*auf*	on (on top of)	*nach*	to, after
		hinter	behind	*von*	from
ohne	without	*in*	in, into	*zu*	to
um	round, at	*neben*	beside, next to	*aus*	out of, from
für	for	*über*	over, above	*bei*	at, with, at the house of
entlang*	along	*unter*	under, below	*seit*	since
wider**		*vor*	in front of	*gegenüber*	opposite
		zwischen	between		

These prepositions take the accusative case only.

These prepositions take either the accusative or the dative case.

These prepositions take the dative case only.

*entlang usually comes after the noun   **wider is an outdated word meaning 'against'

In Category 2, the accusative case is used when there is movement to a place; the dative case is used when there is no movement from one place to another. For example:

Accusative (movement)	Dative (no movement)
Masculine	
*Sie geht **in den** Garten.*	*Sie sitzt **in dem** Garten.*
She goes into the garden.	She is sitting in the garden.
Masculine	
*Die Katze läuft **hinter den** Baum.*	*Die Katze sitzt **hinter dem** Baum.*
The cat runs behind the tree.	The cat is sitting behind the tree.
Feminine	
*Das Auto fährt **unter die** Brücke.*	*Das Auto ist **unter der** Brücke geparkt.*
The car is going under the bridge.	The car is parked under the bridge.
Neuter	
*Ich setze mich **auf das** Sofa.*	*Ich sitze **auf dem** Sofa.*
I sit down on the sofa.	I'm sitting on the sofa.

Quick Test

Try to predict which case should be used in the following sentences, then insert the correct words for 'the' or 'a', as indicated in the brackets: NB: You will need to know the gender of the nouns involved!

1 *Nach _____ Schule gehe ich in _____ Stadt.* (the) (the)

2 *Es gibt eine Drogerie zwischen _____ Bäckerei und _____ Kleidergeschäft.* (the) (the)

3 *Das habe ich für _____ guten Freund gekauft.* (a)

4 *Die Maus ist unter _____ Bett gelaufen.* (the)

5 *Stell das bitte hinter _____ Schrank.* (the)

6 *Wir saßen um _____ Tisch.* (the)

7 *Gestern waren wir in _____ Stadt.* (the)

8 *Ich putze die Fenster mit _____ Schwamm.* (a)

9 *Sie setzte sich neben _____ Mann und _____ Frau.* (the) (the)

10 *Er hat den Brief von _____ guten Freund bekommen.* (a)

Pronouns

As its name suggests, a pronoun is used to replace a noun, e.g.

Der Junge *ist faul.*
The boy is lazy.
masculine noun

Er macht die Hausaufgaben nicht.
He doesn't do the homework.
masculine pronoun

Madonna *singt gut.*
Madonna sings well.
feminine noun

Sie ist sehr berühmt.
She is very famous.
feminine pronoun

Das Mineralwasser *ist kalt.*
The mineral water is cold.
neuter noun

Es schmeckt gut.
It tastes good.
neuter pronoun

Die Schuhe *waren teuer.*
The shoes were dear.
plural noun

Sie haben €200 gekostet.
They cost €200.
plural pronoun

If a pronoun is the subject of a sentence, it is in the nominative case.

If a pronoun is the direct object of a sentence, it is in the accusative case.

If a pronoun is the indirect object of a sentence, it is in the dative case.

If a pronoun follows a preposition, it is either in the accusative or the dative case (see page 96).

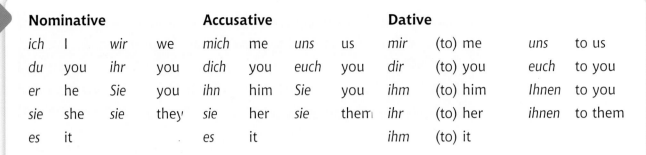

Nominative				Accusative				Dative			
ich	I	wir	we	mich	me	uns	us	mir	(to) me	uns	to us
du	you	ihr	you	dich	you	euch	you	dir	(to) you	euch	to you
er	he	Sie	you	ihn	him	Sie	you	ihm	(to) him	Ihnen	to you
sie	she	sie	they	sie	her	sie	them	ihr	(to) her	ihnen	to them
es	it			es	it			ihm	(to) it		

e.g.

*Wo ist Herr Fischer? Hast du **ihn** gesehen?*

Where is Mr Fischer? Have you seen him? – (direct object pronoun)

*Heute hat Oma Geburtstag. Wir haben **ihr** eine Karte geschickt.*

It's Gran's birthday today. We sent her a card. – (indirect object pronoun)

*Meine Freunde sind **ohne mich** ins Kino gegangen.*

My friends went to the cinema without me. – (The preposition 'ohne' takes the accusative case.)

*Ich will nicht mehr **mit ihnen** ausgehen.*

I don't want to go out with them any more. – (The preposition 'mit' takes the dative case.)

*Anja hat sich **hinter dich** gesetzt.*

Anja sat down behind you.

(The preposition 'hinter' takes the accusative case when there is movement from one place to another.)

*Sie saß die ganze Stunde **hinter dir**.*

She sat behind you the whole period.

(The preposition 'hinter' takes the dative case when there is no movement involved from one place to another.)

Quick Test

Choose the correct pronoun to complete these sentences.
Remember: don't just guess, use your knowledge of cases and prepositions as well as the tables above to help!

1 *Gehst du mit [sie : ihr: wir] ins Kino?*

2 *Ich kenne [ihn : er : ihm] seit Jahren.*

3 *Er setzte sich hinter [ich : mich : mir].*

4 *Ich saß neben [Sie : sie : ihnen].*

5 *Der Film ist toll! Hast du [ihn : es : er] gesehen?*

6 *Ich gehe mit [dich : dir : du].*

Verbs – present tense and perfect tense

Verbs

Verbs are 'doing' or 'being' words, for example 'go', 'work', 'have' and 'is'. They are very important: without a verb you have no sentence!

All verbs have tenses. Tenses tell you when things occur:

- the Present Tense is used to describe what is happening or what happens;
- the Past Tense is used to describe what happened, what has happened or what was happening;
- the Future Tense is used to describe what will happen.

The Present Tense

To form the regular Present Tense, remove -en from the infinitive and add the endings in bold:

gehen	to go
*ich geh**e***	I go (I am going)
*du geh**st***	you go (you are going)
er	he goes (he is going)
*sie geh**t***	she goes (she is going)
es	it goes (it is going)
man	one goes (one is going)
*wir geh**en***	we go (we are going)
*ihr geh**t***	you go (you are going)
*Sie geh**en***	you go (you are going)
sie	they go (they are going)

(*du* – singular, for a child or an adult you know very well, e.g. a relative)

(*man* – for people in general – always takes the same form as *er* / *sie* / *es*)

(*ihr* – the plural of *du*)

(*Sie* – the polite form, for talking to adults; singular and plural)

Some verbs are **irregular**. They change in the *du* and *er* / *sie* / *es* forms, e.g.

sehen	to see
du siehst	you see
er	he
sie sieht	she sees
es	it
man	one

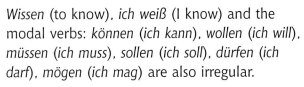

Wissen (to know), *ich weiß* (I know) and the modal verbs: *können* (*ich kann*), *wollen* (*ich will*), *müssen* (*ich muss*), *sollen* (*ich soll*), *dürfen* (*ich darf*), *mögen* (*ich mag*) are also irregular.

fahren	to see
du fährst	you go
er fährt	he goes
sie fährt	she goes
es fährt	it goes
man fährt	one goes

Other irregular verbs add an umlaut, e.g.

Sein (to be) is a very important irregular verb:

ich bin	I am
du bist	you are
er ist	he is
sie ist	she is
es ist	it is
man ist	one is
wir sind	we are
ihr seid	you are
Sie sind	you are
sie sind	they are

Grammar Test 1

Here are some more very common German verbs, and another task for you to complete below!

- *essen*
- *haben*
- *lesen*
- *nehmen*
- *treffen*

Find out what their *du* and *er / sie / es / man* forms are in the Present Tense.

Make a *du* question and an *ich* answer using each of these verbs.

The Past Tense

The Past Tense is used to describe what happened in the past. In German, the Past Tense is divided into the Perfect and the Imperfect Tense.

The Perfect Tense

The Perfect Tense is the tense you use to talk and write about what you did, e.g. last night, at the weekend or during the holidays.

To form the Perfect Tense of most verbs, use the Present Tense of *haben* and a past participle:

ich habe
du hast
er hat
sie hat
es hat
man hat
wir haben
ihr habt
Sie haben
sie haben

Some verbs (usually verbs of movement), use the Present Tense of *sein* instead of *haben*.

In simple sentences and main clauses, the part of *haben* or *sein* goes at the start, and the past participle goes at the end. Think of the Perfect Tense like a sandwich!

ich habe + 'filling' + past participle
ich bin

e.g. **Ich habe** Fußball **gespielt**.
I played football.

Ich bin ins Kino **gegangen**.
I went (have gone) to the cinema.

Past participles

Most past participles start with **ge-**.

Past participles are divided into three groups: weak, strong and mixed.

Weak past participles end in **-t**, and do not change in the middle, e.g.

    machen (to do)   *gemacht* (did / done)

    spielen (to play)   *gespielt* (played)

Strong past participles always end in **-en**, and often change in the middle, e.g.

    gehen (to go)   *gegangen* (went / gone)

    treffen (to meet)   *getroffen* (met)

    but not always, e.g.

    fahren (to go / travel) *gefahren* (went / gone / travelled)

    lesen (to read)   *gelesen* (read)

Mixed past participles end in **-t**, and change in the middle, e.g.

    bringen (to bring / take) *gebracht* (brought / took / taken)

    denken (to think)   *gedacht* (thought)

Some past participles do not start with ge-, e.g.

*Zum Geburtstag **habe ich** einen neuen Computer <u>be</u>**kommen**.*

I got a new computer for my birthday.

***Ich habe** die Weihnachtsferien bei meinen Großeltern <u>ver</u>**bracht**.*

I spent the Christmas holidays at my grandparents'.

***Ich habe** mein Rad **repariert**.*

I repaired my bike.

Quick Test

Fill in the missing auxiliary verb (the part of *haben* or *sein*), then add the correct past participle to the end of these sentences. The verb you have to use is in the infinitive form in brackets.

1 _____ *du den Film* _____? *(sehen)*

2 *Ich* _____ *mir neue Schuhe* _____ *(kaufen)*

3 *Wir* _____ *ins Kino* _____ *(gehen)*

4 *Mein Bruder* _____ *den Hund* _____ *(füttern)*

5 _____ *du mit dem Bus*_____? *(kommen)*

6 *Wir* _____ *Pizza und Salat* _____ *(essen)*

7 *Wie lange* _____ *du dort* _____? *(bleiben)*

8 *Es* _____ *die ganze Zeit* _____ *(regnen)*

9 *Ich* _____ *nach Frankreich* _____ *(fliegen)*

10 _____ *sie [they] ihre Hausaufgaben* _____? *(schreiben)*

Imperfect and future tenses

The Imperfect Tense

The Imperfect Tense is not used as much as the Perfect Tense in Speaking, but you will use some of its more common forms. You will also meet it in Reading.

To form the Imperfect Tense, first split all verbs into three groups: weak, strong and mixed (the same groups as for past participles).

Weak verbs are regular: they don't change in the middle of the verb. To form the Imperfect Tense of a weak verb, take off the **-en** from the infinitive and add these endings:

spielen	to play
*ich spiel**te***	I played / **was playing / used to play**
*du spiel**test***	you played / **were playing / used to play**
*er spiel**te***	he played / **was playing / used to play**
*sie spiel**te***	she played / **was playing / used to play**
*es spiel**te***	it played / **was playing / used to play**
*man spiel**te***	one played / **was playing / used to play**
*wir spiel**ten***	we played / **were playing / used to play**
*ihr spiel**tet***	you played / **were playing / used to play**
*Sie spiel**ten***	you played / **were playing / used to play**
*sie spiel**ten***	they played / **were playing / used to play**

Strong verbs are irregular: there is usually a vowel change in the middle. To form the Imperfect Tense of a strong verb, take off the **-en** from the infinitive, make the vowel change in the middle and add these endings:

gehen	to go
ich ging	I went / was going / used to go
*du ging**st***	you went / were going / used to go
er ging	he went / was going / used to go
sie ging	she went / was going / used to go
es ging	it went / was going / used to go
man ging	one went / was going / used to go
*wir ging**en***	we went / were going / used to go
*ihr ging**t***	you went / were going / used to go
*Sie ging**en***	you went / were going / used to go
*sie ging**en***	they went / were going / used to go

Mixed verbs are a mixture of strong and weak verbs, showing a change in the middle, but using weak endings. To form the Imperfect Tense of a mixed verb, take off the **-en** from the infinitive, make the vowel change in the middle and add these endings.

denken	to think
*ich dach**te***	I thought / **was thinking** / **used to think**
*du dach**test***	you thought / **were thinking** / **used to think**
*er dach**te***	he thought / **was thinking** / **used to think**
*sie dach**te***	she thought / **was thinking** / **used to think**
*es dach**te***	it thought / **was thinking** / **used to think**
*man dach**te***	one thought / **was thinking** / **used to think**
*wir dach**ten***	we thought / **were thinking** / **used to think**
*ihr dach**tet***	you thought / **were thinking** / **used to think**
*Sie dach**ten***	you thought / **were thinking** / **used to think**
*sie dach**ten***	they thought / **were thinking** / **used to think**

The Imperfect Tense of *sein* (to be) is very important, as it is used a lot in both spoken and written German:

ich war	I was
du warst	you were
er war	he was
sie war	she was
es war	it was
man war	one was
wir waren	we were
ihr wart	you were
Sie waren	you were
sie waren	they were

Quick Test

Translate the following Imperfect Tense sentences into English:

1 *Wann warst du in der Stadt?*
2 *Es gab dort nichts zu tun!*
3 *Als ich jung war, hatte ich einen Hund.*
4 *Meine Mutter holte mich vom Bahnhof ab.*
5 *Mein Vater kochte sehr gern.*
6 *Wir gingen auf eine Party.*

e.g.

Wie war die Reise?	How was the journey?
Sie war ganz gut, aber ein bisschen anstrengend!	It was quite good but a bit tiring!
Wo warst du gestern Abend?	Where were you yesterday evening?
Ich war die ganze Zeit zu Hause.	I was at home the whole time.

The Imperfect Tense of *es gibt* (there is / there are) is *es gab* (there was / there were), e.g.

Ich war zwei Wochen in Berlin, und dort gab es so viel zu tun. Das war einfach toll!
I was in Berlin for two weeks and there was so much to do there. It was brilliant!

The Future Tense

This tense is used to describe what is going to happen in the future. To express future plans, use one of these methods:

Method 1
Use the Present Tense with a future time phrase, e.g.

*Am Wochenende **fahre ich** mit meinen Freunden nach Glasgow.*

At the weekend I am going to Glasgow with my friends.

***Ich gehe** heute Abend ins Jugendzentrum.*

I'm going to the youth club tonight.

*In den Sommerferien **fahre ich** mit meinen Eltern in Urlaub nach Italien.*

In the summer holidays I'm going on holiday to Italy with my parents.

Method 2
Use the Present Tense of *werden* (to become) + infinitive.

ich werde	I will
du wirst	You will
er / sie / es / man wird	He / she / it / one will
wir werden + infinitive	We will
	You will
ihr werdet	You / they will
Sie / sie werden	

e.g. ***Wirst du** in zwei Jahren dein Studium **anfangen**?*

Will you start your studies in two years?

*Sonst **werde ich** den Bus **verpassen**.*
Otherwise I will miss the bus.

Notice that in simple sentences and main clauses the infinitive is always the last word, i.e. it gets sent to the end.

If you do want to give details of events which will happen in the (fairly distant) future, then use method 2, as outlined above.

The Conditional
The Conditional is used when we want to say what we WOULD do IF the conditions were right, e.g.

*Ich **wäre** glücklich.* = I would be happy.

*Ich **hätte** eine gute Stelle.* = I would have a good job.

*Ich **möchte** mit Kindern arbeiten.* = I would like to work with children.

*Ich **könnte** in Europa wohnen.* = I could live in Europe.

It can also be used to say what you would do:

*Ich **würde** den Sommer in Italien verbringen.* = I would spend the summer in Italy.

*Wir **würden** ins Konzert gehen.* = We would go to the concert.

*Er **würde** lieber lange schlafen.* = He would prefer to have a long lie in.

*Sie **würden** öfter die Oma besuchen.* = They would visit grandma more often.

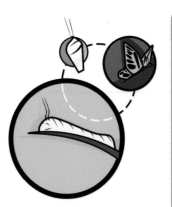

Quick Test

Choose the correct part of *werden* for the following sentences:

1 *Nächstes Jahr [werde : werden : wird] wir nach Amerika fliegen.*

2 *Was [wirst : wird : werdet] du machen?*

3 *Ich [wirst : werde : wird] ein gutes Zeugnis bekommen.*

4 *In zehn Jahren [wird : wirst ; werde] er eine Glatze haben.*

Now translate the sentences into English.

Separable verbs, reflexive verbs and adjectives

Separable verbs

Separable verbs are different from other verbs: they have a separable prefix (e.g. *mit, vor, ab, an, auf, aus, bei, nach, los, zu, um, vorbei* or *zurück*).

The infinitives of separable verbs are used like any other infinitives, e.g.

> *Möchtest du morgen **mitkommen**?*
> Would you like to come with me / us tomorrow?

> *Soll ich morgen früh bei dir **vorbeikommen**?*
> Should I call by at your house tomorrow morning?

The prefix separates from its verb and stands on its own at the end of simple sentences and main clauses, e.g.

> *Wann **kommst** du in Köln **an**?*
> When are you arriving in Cologne?

> *Mein Vati **holt** mich nach der Disko **ab**.*
> My Dad's picking me up after the disco.

Like all other verbs, separable verbs can be regular or irregular, and in the Past Tenses can be weak, strong or mixed. The **ge-** part of the past participle of a separable verb is sandwiched in the middle, e.g. *abgemacht, ferngesehen, mitgebracht.*

Quick Test

Look at the infinitive in the brackets and complete the sentence with the correct version of the separable verb:

Present Tense:

1 *Ich _____ morgens um 7 Uhr _____.* (aufstehen)

2 *Herr Maier _____ heute nachmittag _____.* (zurückkommen)

3 *_____ Sie bitte die Tür _____!* (zumachen)

Perfect Tense:

4 *Die Gäste haben Geschenke _____.* (mitbringen)

5 *Der Bus ist an mir _____.* (vorbeifahren)

6 *Die Passagiere sind am Marktplatz _____.* (aussteigen)

Reflexive verbs

Reflexive verbs are associated with things you do to yourself (e.g. wash, shower, comb your hair, get dressed, get changed).

- Most reflexive verbs are used with accusative (direct) reflexive pronouns:

mich	myself
dich	yourself
sich	himself / herself / itself / oneself
uns	ourselves
euch	yourselves
sich	themselves / yourself (polite), e.g.

Ich wasche mich.
I get washed. (from the verb *sich waschen* – to get washed)

Er zieht sich an.
He gets dressed. (from the verb *sich anziehen* – to get dressed)

Wir fühlen uns hier sehr wohl.
We feel at home here. (from the verb *sich fühlen* – to feel)

- Some reflexive verbs use dative (indirect) reflexive pronouns instead:

mir	myself
dir	yourself
sich	himself / herself / itself / oneself
uns	ourselves
euch	yourselves
sich	themselves / yourself (polite), e.g.

Ich wasche mir die Hände.
I wash my hands. (from the verb *sich die Hände waschen* – to wash one's hands)

Ich putze mir die Zähne.
I clean my teeth. (from the verb *sich die Zähne putzen* – to clean one's teeth)

Das kann ich mir vorstellen!
I can imagine! (from the verb *sich vorstellen* – to imagine)

- In the Imperfect and Perfect Tenses, reflexive verbs behave as normal verbs, e.g.

Ich habe mich gewaschen, und dann habe ich mich im Schlafzimmer angezogen.
I had a wash and then I got dressed in the bedroom.

Quick Test

Using these infinitives of reflexive verbs, write an account of a typical school morning, e.g.

sich waschen — to get washed (wash myself) = *Ich wasche mich*

1	*sich die Zähne putzen*	(to brush your teeth)
2	*sich anziehen*	(to get dressed)
3	*sich kämmen*	(to comb your hair)
4	*sich schminken* optional!	(to put on make-up)
5	*sich beeilen*	(to hurry up)
6	*sich treffen mit*	(to meet)

Now use the same verbs to give an account of what you did last Monday morning. Remember – use the Perfect Tense.

Adjectives

An adjective is a describing word, e.g. 'large', 'blue', 'modern', 'exciting'. In German, when an adjective comes after the noun it describes, it has no ending, e.g.

Die Schule ist altmodisch. The school is old fashioned.
Der Junge ist gutaussehend. The boy is good-looking.
Sie ist sehr intelligent. She is very intelligent.
Das Kind ist hübsch. The child is pretty / lovely.

But when an adjective comes before the noun it describes, it has an ending. Its ending depends on the noun's gender, case, number and article:

gender	case	number	article
masculine?	nominative?	singular?	'the' (the definite article)?
feminine?	accusative?	plural?	'a' (the indefinite article)?
neuter?	genitive?		'not a'/'no' (*kein ...*)?
	dative?		no article (adjective stands on its own)? e.g. *braune Schuhe*

The tables below show which ending to attach to the adjectives.

Table 1 – *der, die, das*

	M	F	NT	PL
NOM	**-e** *der alte Mann*	**-e** *die schöne Frau*	**-e** *das nette Kind*	**-en** *die klugen Kinder*
ACC	**-en** *Kennst du den alten Mann?*	**-e** *Das ist für die schöne Frau.*	**-e** *ohne das nette Kind*	**-en** *für die klugen Kinder*
GEN	**-en** *der Wagen des alten Mannes*	**-en** *das Haus der schönen Frau*	**-en** *wegen des netten Kindes*	**-en** *trotz der klugen Kinder*
DAT	**-en** *mit dem alten Mann*	**-en** *außer der schönen Frau*	**-en** *mit dem netten Kind*	**-en** *mit den klugen Kindern*

Table 2 – *ein, kein, mein, dein, sein, ihr, unser, euer, Ihr, ihr*

	M	F	NT	PL
NOM	-er ein rot**er** Apfel	-e eine gelb**e** Banane	-es ein kalt**es** Getränk	-en meine alt**en** Schuhe
ACC	-en Ich habe einen neu**en** Bleistift gekauft.	-e Haben Sie eine weiß**e** Katze?	-es Haben Sie ein modern**es** Haus?	-en Für seine klein**en** Schwestern
GEN	-en wegen eines schlimm**en** Unfalls	-en trotz einer schlecht**en** Note	-en während eines lang**en** Konzerts	-en wegen unserer alt**en** Nachbarn
DAT	-en mit einem klein**en** Löffel	-en von einer gut**en** Freundin	-em mit ihrem schnell**en** Auto	-en von unseren amerikanisch**en** Freunden

Table 3 – 'Free-standing' adjectives (e.g. 'good' news, 'brown' bread)

	M	F	NT	PL
NOM	-er rot**er** Lippenstift	-e kalt**e** Milch	-es warm**es** Wasser	-e rot**e** Lippen
ACC	-en Ich habe grün**en** Lidschatten gekauft.	-e Haben Sie weiß**e** Schokolade?	-es Haben Sie frisch**es** Obst?	-e für neu**e** Fußballschuhe
GEN	-en wegen stark**en** Regens	-er trotz all**er** Gelegenheit	-en trotz kalt**en** Wetters	-er wegen schlimm**er** Nachrichten
DAT	-em mit braun**em** Zucker	-er Toast mit kalorienarm**er** Margarine	-em aus frisch**em** Gemüse	-en mit klein**en** Kindern

Quick Test

Match the beginnings of the sentences (1–6) to the endings (a–f) to make sentences which contain the correct adjective ending:

1 *Das neue Auto ...*

2 *Wegen starken Verkehrs ...*

3 *Der Zug ist ...*

4 *Der Spielplatz ist für ...*

5 *Ich esse gern ...*

6 *Ich komme mit meiner besten Freundin ...*

a) *durch den langen Tunnel gefahren.*

b) *Brot mit gekochtem Schinken.*

c) *die kleinen Kinder.*

d) *ist ein Mercedes.*

e) *zur Schule.*

f) *hat der Bus zwanzig Minuten Verspätung.*

Inversion and subordinate clauses

Inversion

In a German sentence, the verb is the second 'idea' or 'piece of information' given in a sentence, so it is placed in second position.

For example: *Ich schwimme gern*. In this example, it is easy to identify the verb, as it is the second word in the sentence.

However, if we add more information to the sentence, we have to reorganise the word order. For example:

Im Sommer schwimme ich gern.
1st idea   2nd idea

i.e. we have to move the verb to become the second idea in the sentence. *Im Sommer* is the first idea – the idea of time.

Look at the following examples of the verb being the second idea in the sentence:

1st	2nd	3rd
Mein Bruder	*liest*	*die Zeitung jeden Tag.*
My brother	reads	the paper every day.
Meine Mutter und mein Vater	*sehen*	*oft fern.*
My mother and my father	watch	TV often.
Ich	*gehe*	*manchmal in die Disko.*
I	go	to the disco sometimes.
Es	*gibt*	*viel zu tun in der Stadt.*
There	is	lots to do in the town.

You also apply this second position rule when there is more than one verb in the sentence, e.g. in the Perfect or Future Tenses or with modal verbs. This time, the changing verb is the second position verb. The changing verb is the one which you alter according to the person / thing doing the action (i.e. according to the subject of the sentence), e.g.

*Ich **kann** nicht gut **singen**.*   I can't sing well.
*Er **hat** ein neues Auto **gekauft**.*   He has bought a new car.
  changing verbs   non-changing verbs

Study these further examples:

	1st	2nd	3rd
Perfect Tense	Ja, und dazu	hat	er einen Hut gekauft. Yes, and he also bought a hat.
Future Tense	Nächstes Jahr	werden	wir Verwandte in Kanada besuchen. Next year we will visit relatives in Canada.
Modal verb	Jeden Tag	muss	ich meinen Hund füttern. I have to feed my dog every day.

Quick Test

Start the sentences with the word(s) underlined and alter the word order accordingly:

1 Ich gehe <u>oft</u> einkaufen.

2 Er spielt <u>ab und zu</u> Tennis.

3 Meine Freunde gehen <u>jeden Freitag</u> schwimmen.

4 Sie arbeitet im Sportgeschäft <u>zweimal pro Woche</u>.

5 Ich muss <u>jeden Abend</u> Vokabeln lernen.

6 Ich habe mir <u>letzte Woche</u> eine neue Hose gekauft.

Subordinate clauses

A subordinate clause is part of a sentence.

Ich war glücklich, **als ich jung war**.
I was happy **when I was young**.

The part of the sentence in bold is a subordinate clause.

A subordinate clause starts with a subordinating conjunction, e.g.

wenn	whenever, if
wie	how
weil	because
bevor	before
als	when (in the past)
ehe	before
da	since (because)
nachdem	after
ob	whether
soweit	as far (as ...)
obwohl	although
sooft	as often (as ...)
seit	since (a period of time)
sobald	as soon as
während	while
dass	that

• If you start a sentence in German with one of these subordinating conjunctions, the verb must go to the end of that clause, e.g.

Wenn das Wetter gut **ist** ...
subordinating conjunction
verb to end

If the weather's good ...

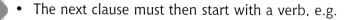

- The next clause must then start with a verb, e.g.

1st clause	2nd clause	
Wenn das Wetter gut **ist,**	**spiele** ich Tennis.	If the weather's good, I play tennis.
subordinating conjunction	verb, comma, verb	

You must always apply the 'verb–comma–verb' rule whenever you start a sentence with any of these subordinating conjunctions.

- If you use a subordinating conjunction in the middle of a sentence, it sends the verb to the end of that clause only (i.e. it does not affect the previous word order), e.g.

normal word order   subordinate clause

Wir spielen heute Tennis, **weil** *das Wetter schön ist.*

                    subordinating conjunction

                  We are playing tennis today because the weather is nice.

- When you have a subordinate clause at the beginning of the sentence, you can still apply the 'verb–comma–verb' rule, even when you have more than one verb in the clause. This time you put the 'changing verb' from clause 1 to the end of that clause (before the comma) – like this:

           clause 1

Da ich meine Hausaufgaben nicht **gemacht**   **habe,** ...

                past participle 'changing verb'

                  Because I've not done my homework, ...

and clause 2's 'changing verb' now comes next

                clause 2

Da ich meine Hausaufgaben nicht gemacht **habe,**   **werde** *ich* ...

            'changing verb', comma 'changing verb'

        We are playing tennis today because the weather is nice.

and the other verb(s) in clause 2 go to the end:

                clause 2

Da ich meine Hausaufgaben nicht **gemacht**   **habe,**   **werde** *ich nicht* **ausgehen** **können.**

        past participle 'changing verb', comma 'changing verb'   other verbs in clause 2

       Because I've not done my homework, I will not be able to go out.

So the rule for sentences containing a subordinate clause is: 'changing verb–comma–changing verb'.

Perfect

Als wir in Deutschland **gewohnt**   **haben,**   **haben** *wir oft Schwarzbrot* **gegessen.**

              past participle   'changing verb'   'changing verb'   past participle

When we lived in Germany, we often ate rye bread.

Future

Wenn du deine Hausaufgaben nicht **machen wirst,**   **wirst** *du schlechte Noten* **bekommen.**

                 infinitive   'changing verb'   'changing verb'   infinitive

If you don't do your homework, you'll get poor grades.

Modal

Sobald ich meine Arbeit fertig **machen**   **kann,**   **komme** *ich zur Party!*

                 infinitive   'changing verb'   'changing verb'

As soon as I can finish my work, I'm coming to the party!

Quick Test

Can you unjumble the rest of these sentences? It's easier than you think! Use the grammar rule above to help you. Remember to insert the comma in the right place!

1 *Da ich [habe : gehe : ich : kein : nicht : aus : Geld]*

2 *Ich lerne gern Deutsch [ist : Grammatik : einfach : die : so : weil]*

3 *Wenn das Wetter [spielen : gern : wir : Fußball : gut : ist]*

4 *Ich war noch hungrig [ich : gefrühstückt : obwohl : hatte : schon]*

Make up four other sentences like the ones above. Remember to ask your teacher to check them.

Some basic language

Time – Manner – Place

Always put the information in your sentences in this order:

Time (T)	before	Manner (M)	before	Place (P)
'when'?		'how'?		'where'?
oft		zu Fuß		Berlin
jedes Jahr		mit dem Zug		Schottland
am Montag				hier

e.g.

Ich fahre **nach Oban**.　　　(P)

Ich fahre **nächste Woche**.　　(T)

Ich fahre **mit dem Zug**.　　　(M)

becomes: Ich fahre **nächste Woche mit dem Zug nach Oban**.

　　　　　　　　　　　　T　　　　　M　　　P

Even if one piece of the TMP information is not in your sentence, the rule still applies, i.e.

　　　T before M　　T before P　　M before P

e.g.

Er geht **zur Schule**.

Er geht **zu Fuß**.

becomes: Er geht zu Fuß zur Schule.

Quick Test

Highlight the Time phrases in green, the Manner places in red and the Place phrases in yellow in these sentences:

1　Gestern sind wir langsam nach Hause gekommen.

2　Ich gehe oft mit meinen Freunden ins Kino.

3　Jeden Morgen ist der Lehrer schlechter Laune in der Mathestunde.

4　Nachmittags kommen die Kinder glücklich nach Hause.

5　Um elf Uhr ist Anja müde ins Bett gegangen.

6　Als ich jung war, ging ich gern zu meiner Oma.

Um ... Zu ...

Um ... zu ... means 'in order to ...'.

- In English, we can often leave out the words 'in order' without changing the meaning of the sentence.

- In German, always use *um ... zu ...* (like the bread in a sandwich) plus a verb in the infinitive, to communicate 'in order to', e.g.

Ich arbeite in einem Supermarkt, um Geld zu **verdienen**.

       comma   infinitive after *zu*

I work in a supermarket in order to earn cash.

Um fit zu **bleiben** , *spiele ich regelmäßig Squash.*

   infinitive comma after infinitive

To stay fit, I play squash regularly.

Quick Test

Make the two sentences into one, by using: *um ... zu ...*

Example: *Ich gehe joggen. Ich bleibe fit. = Ich gehe joggen, um fit zu bleiben.*

1 *Klaus macht immer seine Hausaufgaben. Er bekommt gute Noten.*

2 *Ich habe einen Nebenjob. Ich verdiene Geld.*

3 *Viele Leute kommen in die Stadt. Sie suchen Arbeitsplätze.*

4 *Opa trägt eine Brille. Er sieht besser.*

5 *Ich esse viel Obst und Gemüse. Ich bleibe gesund.*

6 *Vater und Mutter gehen ins Theater. Sie sehen ein neues Theaterstück.*

Numbers

0 null	13 dreizehn	26 sechsundzwanzig
1 eins	14 vierzehn	27 siebenundzwanzig
2 zwei	15 fünfzehn	28 achtundzwanzig
3 drei	16 sechzehn	29 neunundzwanzig
4 vier	17 siebzehn	30 dreißig
5 fünf	18 achtzehn	31 einunddreißig
6 sechs	19 neunzehn	32 zweiunddreißig
7 sieben	20 zwanzig	33 dreiunddreißig
8 acht	21 einundzwanzig	34 vierunddreißig
9 neun	22 zweiundzwanzig	35 fünfunddreißig
10 zehn	23 dreiundzwanzig	36 sechsunddreißig
11 elf	24 vierundzwanzig	37 siebenunddreißig
12 zwölf	25 fünfundzwanzig	38 achtunddreißig

39 neununddreißig	63 dreiundsechzig	87 siebenundachtzig
40 vierzig	64 vierundsechzig	88 achtundachtzig
41 einundvierzig	65 fünfundsechzig	89 neunundachtzig
42 zweiundvierzig	66 sechsundsechzig	90 neunzig
43 dreiundvierzig	67 siebenundsechzig	91 einundneunzig
44 vierundvierzig	68 achtundsechzig	92 zweiundneunzig
45 fünfundvierzig	69 neunundsechzig	93 dreiundneunzig
46 sechsundvierzig	70 siebzig	94 vierundneunzig
47 siebenundvierzig	71 einundsiebzig	95 fünfundneunzig
48 achtundvierzig	72 zweiundsiebzig	96 sechsundneunzig
49 neunundvierzig	73 dreiundsiebzig	97 siebenundneunzig
50 fünfzig	74 vierundsiebzig	98 achtundneunzig
51 einundfünfzig	75 fünfundsiebzig	99 neunundneunzig
52 zweiundfünfzig	76 sechsundsiebzig	
53 dreiundfünfzig	77 siebenundsiebzig	100 hundert
54 vierundfünfzig	78 achtundsiebzig	101 hunderteins
55 fünfundfünfzig	79 neunundsiebzig	
56 sechsundfünfzig	80 achtzig	200 zweihundert
57 siebenundfünfzig	81 einundachtzig	300 dreihundert
58 achtundfünfzig	82 zweiundachtzig	
59 neunundfünfzig	83 dreiundachtzig	1000 tausend
60 sechzig	84 vierundachtzig	2000 zweitausend
61 einundsechzig	85 fünfundachtzig	
62 zweiundsechzig	86 sechsundachtzig	

Time

Days

Montag
Dienstag
Mittwoch
Donnerstag
Freitag
Samstag / Sonnabend (North German)
Sonntag

Seasons

Im Frühling	in spring
Im Sommer	in summer
Im Herbst	in autumn
Im Winter	in winter

Months

Januar
Februar
März
April
Mai
Juni
Juli
August
September
Oktober
November
Dezember

Time

Wie spät ist es? /	What time is it? /
Wieviel Uhr ist es?	What's the time?

Es ist ...	It's ...
ein Uhr	one o'clock
vier Uhr	four o'clock
zwölf Uhr	twelve o'clock
fünf nach eins	five past one
zehn nach zwei	ten past two
Viertel nach drei	quarter past three
zwanzig nach vier	twenty past four
fünfundzwanzig nach fünf	twenty-five past five
halb sechs***	half past five
fünfundzwanzig vor sechs	twenty-five to six
zwanzig vor sieben	twenty to seven
Viertel vor acht	quarter to eight
zehn vor neun	ten to nine
fünf vor zehn	five to ten
Mittag	midday
Mitternacht	midnight

Top Tip

***Half past: Remember that in German, you have to think that it is 'half towards' the next hour, so *halb sechs* = half towards six = half past five. When you are saying 'one o'clock' use '*ein Uhr*', but with all other times to and past one, it becomes '*eins*', e.g. *zehn vor eins, Viertel nach eins* ...

Quick Test

Write out the following times:

1 Half past nine.
2 Ten past six.
3 Half past eight.
4 Twenty to twelve.
5 Quarter to eleven.
6 Twenty-five past ten.
7 Quarter past three.
8 Half past twelve.

Put the following times into English:

1 *Viertel nach sieben.*
2 *Halb drei.*
3 *Viertel vor vier.*
4 *Fünfundzwanzig nach elf.*
5 *Halb eins.*
6 *Viertel nach zwölf.*
7 *Zehn vor sechs.*
8 *Halb elf.*

Writing

Model folios 1

Features of a good folio essay

- The title should be more than just a word, e.g. *Schule*, but should expand on that word to indicate what you are going to write about, e.g.

  Was ich von der Schule halte (What I think about school)

- Your essay should demonstrate some structure right from the start. How can you do this? Well, as with any essay, it has to be planned before you start writing it. What aspects of the topic have you decided to include, and which (if any) have you decided to leave out? Then decide on the order in which you are going to bring in each of these points.

- The best way to demonstrate that there is a structure to your essay is to use certain phrases which will flag up what is coming next. This can be done with phrases like this:

Erstens	First of all
Zweitens	Secondly
Anschließend	Then
Die Vorteile sind	The advantages are
Die Nachteile sind	The disadvantages are
Im Großen und Ganzen	All in all
Zum Schluss	Finally

- To grab the reader's (in this case, the examiner's) attention, you could start your essay with a statement like: '*Die Schule? Ich hasse die Schule!*' or '*Die Ferien? Ich liebe die Ferien!*' or '*Freizeitjobs? Ich habe die Nase voll!*' (I'm sick to death!).

- Ensure that you express yourself clearly. You will be able to assess whether you have managed this when you read over the finished essay.

- Try to move beyond single-clause, simple sentences by using conjuctions like *weil, wenn, obwohl*. (See Grammar section, page 108.) This allows you to develop your opinions or arguments, resulting in a more interesting text for the reader. Remember, you want to show off that you can handle more complicated sentences!

- Always try to include some more sophisticated or complex vocabulary in your essay to show that you have moved beyond very simple language.

- Punctuation is important, so remember to double check for missed commas, full stops, etc.

- Remember that detail adds interest and you can do this by using adjectives. As you are aware, there are several different adjective endings to choose from, so it's a good idea to work out and practise some useful examples, e.g.

  Im Winter trage ich **meine** *dicke Jacke und meine* **warmen** *Handschuhe.*

- It is important that you demonstrate that you can use at least two tenses in a credit essay and use them in the correct context. The Present Tense is straightforward. Remember that the Perfect Tense is used for completed actions in the past, and the Imperfect Tense is for on-going, routine actions and for description.

- The use of prepositions is an area where you can demonstrate that you have a sound grasp of grammar. As with verbs, prepare a few examples to include, e.g.

  Am Wochenende bin ich mit der Clique **in die Stadt** *gegangen.*

  In der Stadt *war viel los.*

- The guideline word count for General is 50–100 words, and for Credit is 100–200 words. Remember that this is a guideline, so don't worry if you are slightly over or under these amounts. However, you do not want to be too much over, as the more you write, the more mistakes you are likely to make.

- Finally, as with all work, it is important to present an essay which is legible, properly spaced and looks neat. Leave the fancy pens at home and use only black or blue.

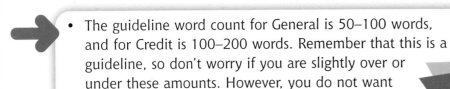

Top Tip

It really is worth the time spent on redrafting your essays when your teacher returns a corrected version. If you incorporate the corrections and suggested improvements, you really will have the 'Perfect Essay'!

Sample essay 1

Read through and listen to this Credit essay.

Wie ich meine Sommerferien verbringe

Ich freue mich immer auf die Sommerferien. Sechs Wochen ohne meine Lehrer und die vielen Hausaufgaben sind absolut fantastisch!

Normalerweise fahre ich mit meinen Eltern und meiner Schwester in Urlaub an die See – entweder nach Portugal oder nach Italien. Wir fliegen immer, weil es praktisch und billig ist, und weil man schnell dahin kommt. Leider müssen wir immer in den Schulferien fahren, wenn das Wetter sehr heiß ist und viele Touristen unterwegs sind.

Auf der einen Seite ist es schön, mit den Eltern in Urlaub zu fahren, weil sie fast alles bezahlen. Auf der anderen Seite finde ich es nervend, wenn sie so viele Sehenswürdigkeiten besichtigen. Das ist stinklangweilig!

Mein Lieblingsurlaub war vor zwei Jahren, als ich dreizehn war. Wir haben drei Wochen auf einem Campingplatz in Südportugal verbracht. Da haben wir eine nette Familie aus Frankreich kennengelernt. Ich habe mich mit der ältesten Tochter angefreundet und wir haben uns gut verstanden. Natürlich waren wir traurig, als der Urlaub vorbei war.

Mein Traumurlaub wäre in Australien. Ich würde gern eine Tour durch den Kontinent machen, um die Landschaft und die wilden Tiere zu sehen.

Kurz gesagt fahre ich gern in Urlaub, und ich möchte so viele Länder wie möglich sehen.

Quick Test

1 How many examples of subordinate clauses can you find in this piece?

2 How many examples of the Conditional can you find?

Now try to write four sentences – one using a 'starter' phrase, one using subordinate word order, one using the Imperfect and one using the Conditional.

How good is this essay?

Structure

It is clear that this essay is organised into sections, each one dealing with one particular aspect of the topic. The first paragraph states how the writer feels; the next three deal with separate aspects of holidays with the family; paragraph five deals with what a dream holiday would be like for the writer, while the last paragraph is introduced by a phrase which indicates that a summary is to follow.

Grammar

The writer demonstrates that they can use not only the Present Tense, but also the Perfect, Imperfect and the Conditional. Subordinate word order has also been used.

Vocabulary

The range of vocabulary includes basic sound, correct items, as well as some 'showy' words such as *Sehenswürdigkeiten* and *unterwegs*. The writer has made use of some good starter phrases such as *normalerweise* and *auf der anderen Seite*.

Beyond the basics

The writer has elaborated on many points, giving lots of detail and reasons for likes and dislikes.

Sample essay 2 18

Wie ich meinen Geburtstag feiere

Wann ich Geburtstag habe? Im Juli! Das finde ich toll, weil es viele Möglichkeiten gibt, meinen Geburtstag zu feiern.

Wenn das Wetter an meinem Geburtstag schön ist, gehe ich gerne tagsüber mit der Clique zum Strand, wo wir den ganzen Tag schwimmen und Volleyball spielen. Das macht mir echt Spaß! Auf der anderen Seite, wenn das Wetter schlecht ist, gehen wir zum Eisstadion.

Normalerweise gebe ich keine Party – das ist für kleine Kinder! Es macht viel mehr Spaß, mit meinen Freunden auszugehen. Dieses Jahr, zum Beispiel, wollen wir am Abend zur Bowlingbahn gehen. Da gibt es eine gute Atmosphäre, und außerdem können wir den ganzen Abend dort verbringen.

Was ich zum Geburtstag bekommen möchte? Was mir am besten gefällt, ist Geld oder CD's geschenkt zu bekommen. Letztes Jahr habe ich ein fantastisches T-Shirt von meiner Schwester in der Schweiz bekommen. Dieses Jahr möchte ich wieder Geld, dann kann ich mir kaufen, was ich will.

Mein bester Geburtstag war vor drei Jahren, als ich mit meiner Familie auf Urlaub in Italien war. Wir haben tagsüber am Schwimmbecken gelegen, haben eiskalte Getränke getrunken und als es zu heiß wurde, sind wir geschwommen. Am Abend sind wir in ein kleines Restaurant gegangen, wo es fantastische Pizzen gab. Mensch, war das gut!

Insgesamt würde ich sagen, dass Geburtstage mir viel Spaß machen und ich freue mich auf nächsten Juli!

How good is this essay?

This is a Credit essay, for the following reasons:

- It is clearly structured, with an introduction, a conclusion and different aspects covered in separate paragraphs.
- Reasons and opinions are given, which make the essay interesting.
- There is a range of tenses – Present, Perfect and Imperfect, as well as an example of the Conditional.
- There are instances of subordinate clauses, inversion and starter phrases.
- Good use of adjectives and prepositions.

Top Tip

Look at the middle four paragraphs, between the introduction and the conclusion. Can you think of a title for each of them? When you have done this, it will illustrate how the essay has been constructed.

Quick Test

How many examples can you find in the essay of:

1 time phrases?

2 adjectival phrases?

How to prepare for folio assessments

The following tips will help you prepare in manageable steps:

- Once you have all the necessary grammar, vocabulary and phrases from your class work, decide which points you are going to include and which you are going to omit from the essay.
- Decide on the structure of the essay, remembering that it must have a short introduction and a conclusion, as well as the main part ordered in a logical sequence, e.g. WHEN is your birthday, WHAT you like to do, WHAT presents you like to get, and YOUR BEST EVER birthday.
- When you have written the first draft, your teacher will give you useful comments and guidance on how the essay can be improved. Obviously, it makes sense to hand these drafts in by the deadline, so that you have the maximum amount of time to work on it when you get it back. Avoid the 'last minute dash'!
- Redrafting as soon as possible is a good idea, as your teacher's advice will be fresh in your memory. Doing it in different ways can make this less tedious – type it up, highlighting particular phrases you want to remember. You can also edit the piece easily. Alternatively, write each paragraph on a separate sheet of paper, and literally deal with the essay in small chunks, instead of being overwhelmed by the whole thing. In this way, you can learn each paragraph by heart, and even ask a parent or friend to listen to you reciting it while they follow your text!
- When you feel confident, try writing the essay at home under test conditions – keeping to 40 minutes, no notes, dictionary only.
- AVOID using the dictionary during the actual timed test in class, unless you have simply forgotten a particular word that you intended to include, or to check on correct spelling. By this stage, you should be well enough prepared to know exactly what you want to write.

Notes

Answers

Personal language

Self 1

Quick Test (p. 11)

1 Sometimes my sister is lazy, but she's always nice.
2 I am quite small and have shoulder-length red hair.
3 My brother is often annoying and in a bad mood.
4 I think my sister is a bit silly.
5 I am really good-looking!

Self 2

Quick Test (p. 13)

1 *Mein Geburtstag ist am … / Ich habe am … Geburtstag.*
2 *am achten Mai / am 8. Mai.*
am sechsten Oktober / am 6. Oktober.
am dreißigsten November / am 30. November.
am zwölften Dezember / am 12. Dezember.
am sechsundzwanzigsten März / am 26. März .

Self 3

Exercise 1 (p. 14)

GERMAN	ENGLISH
lockige Haare	**curly hair**
grüne Augen	**green eyes**
ziemlich dick	**quite fat**
gutaussehend	**good looking**
glatte Haare	**straight hair**
launisch	**moody**
egoistisch	**selfish**
vernünftig	**sensible**
doof	**daft / silly**
Ich bin Schottin.	**I am Scottish (female).**
Ich habe keine Geschwister.	**I have no brothers or sisters / I am an only child.**
Ich wohne in Glenrothes.	**I live in Glenrothes.**
Ich bin selten schlecht gelaunt.	**I am rarely in a bad mood.**
dünn	**thin**
Das liegt im Süden.	**It's in the south.**
Ich bin sehr sportlich.	I'm very sporty.
Ich habe blaue Augen.	I've got blue eyes.
Ich habe kurze blonde Haare.	I've got short blond hair.
Ich bin ziemlich groß und schlank.	I'm quite tall and slim.
Ich bin oft gut gelaunt.	I'm often in a good mood.
Ich bin normalerweise / gewöhnlich freundlich.	I'm usually friendly.

Exercise 2 (p. 15)

1 = T	2 = F	3 = F	4 = T
5 = F	6 = F	7 = T	8 = T
9 = T	10 = T		

Family 1

Quick Test (p. 19)

1 *Polizistin*
2 *Lehrer*
3 *Bäuerin*
4 *Zahnarzt*
5 *Geschäftsfrau*

Exercise 2 (p. 19)

Meine Stiefschwester
Mein Schwager
Mein Cousin / Vetter
Meine Verlobte

Family 2

Quick Test (p. 21)

1 = *i*
2 = *d*
3 = *e*
4 = *f*
5 = *h*
6 = *a*
7 = *j*
8 = *c*
9 = *b*
10 = *g*

Meet Uwe! (p. 21)

1 North Germany.
2 He is called Stephan / he is 21 / lives in Hamelin / is a student / likes playing football.
3 Mother is a librarian, father is an engineer.
4 They are all younger than him.
5 It's annoying!

Family 3

Exercise 1 (p. 22)

GERMAN	ENGLISH
Schwägerin	**sister-in-law**
Töchter	**daughters**
Vetter	**male cousin(s)**
Verlobte	**fiancée**
Opa	**grandad**
Geschwister	**brothers and sisters**
Zwillingsbruder	**twin brother**
Stiefschwester	**stepsister**
Söhne	**sons**
Halbschwester	**half sister**

MALE JOBS	FEMALE JOBS
Pilot	***Pilotin***
Bauer	*Bäuerin*
Zahnarzt	***Zahnärztin***
Lehrer	***Lehrerin***
Krankenpfleger	*Krankenschwester*

Quick Test (p. 23)

- The mother
- The grandfather
- The father
- The mother
- The grandfather
- The grandmother

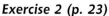

Exercise 2 (p. 23)

FAMILY MEMBER	AGE	PHYSICAL DESCRIPTION	CHARACTER	JOB	ANY OTHER DETAILS
Grandfather	91	Small, a bit fat, has a white beard.	Is very patient and friendly.	Was a police officer.	He was born in Munich.
Grandmother	88	Has short grey hair, green eyes, is 1.45m tall, is slim.	She is lively, really nice and a bit mad.	Was a journalist.	She is Austrian and comes from Vienna.
Father	50	Average height, has short curly hair and wears glasses.	Friendly and laid-back / not strict.	Businessman.	He works for a large company in Linz in Austria.
Mother	46	Pretty, small, has shoulder length black hair and brown eyes.	Sometimes moody when tired, can be really nice but is always strict.	Opera singer.	She is Swiss. She works all over the world. She only works 6 months a year.

Hobbies 1

Quick Test (p. 26)

1 Does piano practice for an hour / does her homework / watches TV / reads in bed.
2 Documentaries and nature programmes.
3 Meets her friends, they go to the shopping centre if they have money and they sometimes go to a party.
4 She plays piano and she likes music programmes on TV.
5 In the summer holidays.

Hobbies 2

Quick Test (p. 29)

1 *freitags*
2 *jeden Monat*
3 *zweimal pro Woche*
4 *im Winter*
5 *im Großen und Ganzen*

Time phrases (p. 29)

normalerweise	**normally / usually**
im Großen und Ganzen	**generally / on the whole**
jeden Tag	**every day**
am Wochenende	**at the weekend**
in den Ferien	**in the holidays**
samstags	**on Saturdays**
nach der Schule	**after school**
am Nachmittag	**in the afternoon**
im Sommer	**in the summer**
einmal pro Woche	**once a week**
jeden Morgen	**every morning**
manchmal	**sometimes**

Hobbies 3

Exercise 1 (p. 30)

Am Wochenende schlafe ich mich gut aus, weil ich von der Schule so müde bin. Zuerst gehe ich in die Stadt, wo ich meine Freunde treffe. Wir gehen in den Park, um Fußball zu spielen. Unsere Mannschaft kann echt gut kicken! Danach gehen wir ins Café, um uns zu erholen. Ich bin Mitglied eines Jugendzentrums und dort spiele ich Tischtennis oder Schach. Manchmal aber faulenze ich nur und sehe fern oder ich lese eine Zeitschrift. Meine Schwester Angela spielt gern mit dem Computer, sieht gern fern und fährt auch gern mit dem Rad.

Exercise 2 (p. 30)

Zeitschriften
Jugendzentrum
einen Film an
eislaufen
faulenze ich

Education 1

Quick Test (p. 35)

1 Chemistry is my favourite subject.
2 I don't like art at all.
3 I go to a comprehensive school.
4 You have to wear a uniform to school.
5 You are not allowed to skate in the corridors.

Education 2

Quick Test (p. 37)

1 = b
2 = d or f
3 = e
4 = a
5 = d or f
6 = c

Education 3

Quick Test (p. 38)

1 *ich besuche*
2 *Latein gefällt mir (gut)*
3 *blöd stinklangweilig*
4 *eine Menge*
5 *normalerweise*
6 *danach*

Exercise 1 (p. 38)

1 On the outskirts of town.
2 She likes it, but it's difficult and complicated.
3 She doesn't have a good relationship with him and he is not good at listening.
4 By train.
5 Drinks Coke, chats to friends.
6 Five of: Does her homework / watches TV for an hour / speaks to friends on the phone / surfs the net / eats her evening meal / reads a magazine / goes to bed at 10.30.

Exercise 2 (p. 39)

1 Three.
2 Likes it when they have badminton, it can often be tiring.
3 French and Latin – they are sometimes complicated.
4 They are the most important subjects.
5 Computer programmer.
6 The teacher is too laid back (lax) and speaks German almost all the time / they learn nothing.
7 History.

Tourist language

Where I live 1

Quick Test (p. 41)

```
N O R D W E S T D E U T S C H L A N D
A s a a O i t h i s h a t a o a r ä o
C t t c H n a e s s r n o f b n b h p
H s h h N k d a k z   k c é b d e e p
T c a b Z a t t o i   s k   y e i   e
K h u o I u   e m t   r t   r t l
L o s d M f   r m e   a s   a s h
U t   e M s   e l     u z   a
B t   n E z   r l     m i   u
  l     R e           e     m   s
  a       n                 m
  n       t                 e
  d       r                 r
          u
          m
```

Where I live 2

Quick Test (p. 43)

1 You can go jogging in the many parks.
2 There is a brilliant music shop very close by.
3 The hotel is in a quiet location.
4 It's a good place to relax.

Quick Test (p. 45)

1 *(e)*	5 *(c)*
2 *(h)*	6 *(g)*
3 *(f)*	7 *(b)*
4 *(a)*	8 *(d)*

Where I live 3

Exercise 1 (p. 46)

Doppelhaus
nicht weit von
ruhigen
ersten Stock
eine Terrasse
grillen
einen Schreibtisch
Hausaufgaben mache
Auf dem Schrank
viele Fotos
auf dem land

Exercise 3 (p. 47)

Fairground	No
Car factory	Yes
Airport	Yes
Ice rink	No
Market	Yes
Multiplex	No
Town hall	Yes

Quick Test (p. 47)

1 *Ich freue mich darauf.*
2 *Das müssen wir unbedingt sehen.*
3 *Eine Dreiviertelstunde*
4 *Von da oben …*
5 *Jede Menge Souvenirs und Postkarten*

Transport 1

Quick Test (p. 49)

1 *der Fahrkartenautomat*
2 *die Monatskarte*
3 *eine Panne*
4 *ein Reisepass*
5 *die Fahrgäste*

Transport 2

Quick Test (p. 51 (Sample answer)

Liebe Ursula,
Im Juli bin ich mit meiner Familie mit dem Auto nach Tossa de Mar in Spanien gefahren. Die Fähre von Portsmouth nach Bilbao war toll, aber die lange Reise mit dem Auto war so langweilig, und mein Bruder war nervend. Unterwegs haben wir in einer kleinen Pension übernachtet, wo wir ein schönes Frühstück gegessen haben.
Wir sind am zehnten Juli in Tossa de Mar angekommen. Da haben wir zwei Wochen auf einem großen Campingplatz verbracht. Super!
Viel Grüße,
Deine Angela

Exercise 1 (p. 51)

1 By bus.
2 In Zeebrugge.
3 Her classmates.
4 They had a boat trip on the Rhine.

Transport 3

Exercise 1 (p. 52)

Exercise 2 (p. 53)

Anagrams	German	English
ANOBHBUFSH	*Busbahnhof*	Bus station
FUNKATUS	*Auskunft*	Information
CHRÄLIßECESFH	*Schließfächer*	Lockers
ENAFFHULG	*Flughafen*	Airport
MEEBNSR	*Bremsen*	Brakes
GRUNTHIC	*Richtung*	Direction
DEHÄKGANCP	*Handgepäck*	Hand luggage
UEMUGLNIT	*Umleitung*	Diversion
TRUCKLFDU	*Luftdruck*	Air pressure

Exercise 3 (p. 53)

1 Because of a breakdown, there is a traffic jam on the motorway, heading towards Bonn.
2 Passengers traveling on the 10 o' clock bus to Jena will have to change in Weimar.
3 The Lufthansa flight 765 to New York is three hours late.
4 The A6 is closed to the south of Hanover due to (black) ice.
5 Today, there's a diversion via Klausdorf.
6 Because of the carnival in the town centre, the last buses won't leave until one thirty.

Quick Test (p. 53)

1 Car
2 Bus
3 Plane
4 Train
5 Car
6 Train

Holidays 1

Quick Test (p. 55)

1 *In Porto Pollensa auf Mallorca.*
2 *Ein Einzelzimmer mit Vollpension.*
3 *Ist das Hotel rollstuhlgängig?*

Holidays 2

Quick Test (p. 57)

1 We reserved a double room with toilet and shower.
2 Do you have any spaces available for a tent and a camper-bus?
3 You (plural) have to bring sheets or sleeping bags with you.
4 Dogs are not allowed to come into the hotel.

Holidays 3

Exercise 1 (p. 58)

Guten Abend. Haben Sie reserviert?
Nein, wir haben nicht reserviert. Haben Sie noch Platz frei?
Für wie viele Personen?
Zwei Erwachsene und drei Kinder.
Ja, ich habe einen Platz. Für wie viele Nächte?
Für fünf Nächte. Was kostet das?
€15 pro Person pro Nacht.
Das ist aber teuer! Na gut! Gibt es hier einen Wäscheraum? Unsere Kleider sind schmutzig.
Ja, wir haben einen Wäscheraum. Ihr Zeltplatz ist links vom Wäscheraum.
Aber das finde ich zu laut. Haben Sie andere Zeltplätze?
Es tut mir leid. Das ist der letzte Zeltplatz. Es ist ja 21.00 Uhr!
Ja, ich weiß – wir sind sehr spät angekommen, und es ist dunkel. Haben Sie eine Taschenlampe dabei?
Ja danke, das habe ich – aber ich brauche eine Flasche Gas.
Das können Sie im Supermarkt kaufen. Er ist bis 22.00 Uhr geöffnet.
Dann gehe ich gleich hin.

Quick Test (p. 59)

Do
Collect form from reception.
Use the swimming pool – from 7.00–20.00.
Swim all day.
Pay for bike hire at reception.

Must
Fill in registration form.
Bring bikes back by 21.00.
Use the stairs during a fire alarm.
Show ID on entering dining-room.

Don't
Bring drinks or fast food into the bedrooms.
Play loud music after 11 in the evening.
Shout, sing loudly or make a noise near the bedrooms.
Smoke – either on the ground floor or in the bedrooms.
Use the swimming pool after 8 p.m.
Use the lift during a fire alarm.

Eating out 1

Quick Test (p. 61)

gesund	ungesund
Gurkensalat	*Backfisch mit Pommes frites*
Forelle	*Käsesahnetorte mit Schlagsahne*
Salzkartoffeln	*Drei Kugel Schokoladeneis mit Sahne*
gemischter Salat	*Apfelkuchen*

Eating out 2

Exercise 1 (p. 63)

Present	Perfect
Wir warten schon seit 30 Minuten.	*Das habe ich nicht bestellt!.*
Dieses Gericht ist kalt.	*Wir haben keine Pizza bestellt.*
Das Glas ist schmutzig.	*Man hat einen Fehler gemacht.*
Mir fehlt ein Messer/eine Gabel/ein Löffel.	

Quick Test (p. 63)

1 (W) Have you already ordered?
2 (C) What can you recommend?
3 (C) I'd like to see the menu.
4 (W) For how many people?
5 (C) The fork is dirty.
6 (C) I'll have a Coke with that.
7 (C) Ich habe keine Cola bestellt.
8 (W) Was darf es sein?
9 (W) Schönen Tag noch!
10 (C) Ich bin allergisch gegen käse.

Eating out 3

Exercise 1 (p. 64)

Anagrams	German	English
DRINKS		
DESRULP	*Sprudel*	Fizzy water
OKAKA	*Kakao*	Cocoa
FETSLAPFA	*Apfelsaft*	Apple juice
HEKIFLCEMAF	*Milchkaffee*	White coffee
DILANOEM	*Limonade*	Lemonade
FOODS		
MESPMO TRESFI	*Pommes frites*	Chips
EGRISEPLEIE	*Spiegeleier*	Fried eggs
ROLTARFAKEFTNB	*Bratkartoffeln*	Fried potatoes
TOSTERBOT	*Obsttorte*	Fruit flan
BENESR	*Erbsen*	Peas
REMIHENEB	*Himbeeren*	Raspberries

Exercise 2 (Sample answers) (p. 64)

1 *Wie viele sind Sie?* — *Wir sind vier Personen.*
2 *Raucher oder Nichtraucher?* — *Nichtraucher, bitte.*
3 *Möchten Sie die Speisekarte sehen?* — *Ja, die Speisekarte, bitte.*
4 *Was darf es sein?* — *Ich hätte gern ein Wienerschnitzel.*
5 *Sind Sie Vegetarier?* — *Ja, ich bin Vegetarier.*
6 *Was trinken Sie dazu?* — *Ich trinke eine Limo dazu.*
7 *Ist alles in Ordnung?* — *Ja, danke – alles ist in Ordnung.*
8 *Schönen Tag noch!* — *Danke!*

Exercise 3 (p. 65)

1 Black Forest gateau, 1 apple cake with whipped cream, 2 white coffees. 12 euros 40.
1 Coke, 1 fizzy water, 1 strawberry ice-cream, 1 ice cream sundae. 9 euros 65.
2 cheese omelettes with fried potatoes, 1 apple juice, 1 orange juice. 11 euros 90.
3 fried fish with chips, 1 veal escalope. 19 euros 25.
1 sausage with potato salad, 1 escalope with mushroom sauce with boiled potatoes, 2 mixed salads. 16 euros 45.

Quick Test (p. 65)

1 *Einmal Schinkenbrot und einmal Sprudel.*
2 *Zweimal Pommes mit Mayo und zweimal Kaffee.*
3 *Dreimal Cola und dreimal Tee mit Zitrone.*
4 *Einmal Schokoladentorte und einmal Eis: Erdbeer und Vanille.*
5 *Einmal Eisbecher und einmal Currywurst.*
6 *Einmal Obsttorte mit Schlagsahne und einmal Tee mit Milch.*

Problems

Relationships 3

Exercise 1 (p. 72)

Positive	Negative
ruhig	egoistisch
lieb	verklemmt
aufgeschlossen	geizig
ehrlich	langweilig
geduldig	gemein
sensibel	
vernünftig	
großzügig	

NB schüchtern (shy) could be either positive or negative – you decide!

Exercise 2 (p. 72)

Katja: She's in love with her older brother's friend. She gets on well with her brother, but hasn't dared speak to him about it, for fear he'll laugh at her and it would be so embarrassing. She dreams about him all the time and can't concentrate on her schoolwork and got a bad school report. School just seems boring and difficult. She just wants to go out with him.

Michael: His parents have separated and he lives with his mother. She now has a new boyfriend, who has moved in with them. He has to 'share' his mother with this new man. This man has two children, who come to stay at the weekend. They have to share Michael's bedroom, as the flat is small and he can't stand them. They are untidy, they take his clothes, steal his CDs and want to watch children's TV programmes all the time. Also, he doesn't get on well with his 'new father': he treats him like a child and is strict. He wouldn't let him go to the cinema with his friends last weekend, because he had a lot of homework to do.

Health issues 1

Quick Test (p. 75)

1 *Tabletten*
2 *Pillen*
3 *Verbände*
4 *Pflaster*
5 *Salbe*
6 *Augentropfen*
7 *Saft*
8 *Hustenbonbons*

Health issues 2

Quick Test (p. 76)

1 My arm is sore.
2 My leg is sore.
3 My nose is sore.
4 My eyes are sore.
5 My fingers are sore.
6 My hands are sore.
7 I have a sore throat.
8 I have toothache.
9 I have stomach-ache.
10 I have backache.

Quick Test (p. 77)

1 *tun weh*
2 *tut weh*
3 *tut weh*
4 *tut weh*
5 *tut weh*
6 *tun weh*
7 *tun weh*
8 *tut weh*

Exercise 1 (p. 78)

1 = e
2 = f
3 = d
4 = a
5 = c
6 = b

Exercise 2 (p. 78)

das Handgelenk
der Arm
das Herz
ich habe eine Lebensmittelvergiftung
ich habe mir das Fußgelenk verrenkt
meine Zehe tun weh
mein Auge tut weh
ich habe Ohrenschmerzen
die Nase
die Schulter
mein Ellbogen tut weh
ich habe Rückenschmerzen
der Fuß

Exercise 3 (p. 79)

1 The father has diarrhoea, the mother has constipation and the son has a rash.
2 The breakfast in the guesthouse where they are staying.
3 He says the landlady is horrible, a real witch – but she is the chemist's mother!
4 Take 10 tablets with a litre of water after breakfast, jog to the next village and find another guesthouse.
5 His 80 year-old father gets up at 4 a.m. every day to bake the bread, his 90 year-old mother cooks the jam every afternoon and the eggs are from his beloved uncle's farm.

Health issues 3

Quick Test (p. 79)

GERMAN	ENGLISH
ein wenig	a little / a bit
peinlich	embarrassing
Eier	eggs
leiden	to suffer
Hautausschlag	a rash
wagen	to dare
ablegen	to turn down / refuse
die Wirtin	landlady
böse	nasty; angry
empfehlen	to recommend
damit	so that
Bescheid wissen	to know / to be informed
beliebt	favourite
adieu	goodbye (very final)

Environment 1

Quick Test (p. 81)

1 *die Klimaveränderung* (climate change)
2 *die Autoabgase* (exhaust fumes)
3 *der Meeresspiegel* (sea-level)
4 *die Umweltverschmutzung* (pollution)
5 *das Altglas* (recycled glass)
6 *die Plasiktüte* (plastic bags)

Environment 2

Quick Test (p. 83)

1 To be honest, the main problem is wasting energy.
2 We should travel by public transport.
3 One / We would have to learn it in school.

Exercise 1 (p. 84)

1 *Herr Steinherz*
2 *Frau Grünewald*
3 *Frau Rosenthal*
4 *Frau Grünewald*
5 *Herr Steinherz*
6 *Frau Grünewald*

Exercise 2 (p. 85)

Klaus

Town Pros

Doesn't need a car, public transport so good, especially underground and trams. Cheaper than buying a car, fast and reliable. Doing this helps to protect the environment.

Town Cons

To go for a nice walk, has to take underground to the parks and there is no beach, because Berlin is so far from the coast.

Trude

Country Pros

Quiet and pleasant, no hustle and bustle. Lives on a nature reserve, so rivers are unpolluted, air is clean and endangered species are protected. Trees have not been cut down for new housing.

Country Cons

Nothing to do for young people, especially if you live on a farm. No nightlife, because bus links are bad – last bus from nearest town leaves att 9.30.

Environment 3

Quick Test (p. 85)

1 *und dabei schonen wir die Umwelt.*
2 *Leider gibt es kein Nachtleben.*
3 *Ich wohne auf einem Bauernhof, wo man Bio-Lebensmittel produziert.*
4 *Gibt es überhaupt Nachteile?*
5 *Ich kann mir nicht vorstellen, irgendwo anders als hier in der Stadtmitte Berlins zu wohnen*

One World 1

Quick Test (p. 87)

1 Many Belgians speak French.
2 Asylum-seekers have come from all over the world.
3 Many guest workers are Turkish.
4 Many immigrants come to Germany.

Quick Test (p. 87)

1 *die Dürre = die Überflutung*
2 *der Tod = die Geburt*
3 *die Kenntnisse = die Unwissenheit*
4 *die Liebe = der Hass*
5 *die Einwohner = die Fremden / die Einsiedler*
6 *die Armut = der Reichtum*

One World 2

Quick Test (p. 89)

1 *Die Männer verlassen die Heimat.*
2 *Sie wandern in ein neues Land ein.*
3 *Sie suchen Arbeit.*
4 *Sie arbeiten auf Baustellen.*
5 *Man spricht nur die Muttersprache.*
6 *Sie lernen deutsch.*
7 *Die Familien folgen den Männern.*
8 *Man bringt die eigene Kultur mit.*
9 *Man lebt sich langsam ein.*
10 *Man bemüht sich, die neuen Sitten zu lernen.*
11 *Man versteht sich gut mit den Nachbarn.*

One World 3

Quick Test (p. 90)

1 *Ich habe jede Menge Tanten und Onkeln.*
2 *Wir freuen uns immer darauf!*
3 *Mein Vater hat eine gute Stelle*
4 *Hast du immer noch Verwandte in der Türkei?*
5 *Allerlei Freunde.*

Exercise 1 (p. 90)

Türkisch
Meine Großeltern sind 1967 aus der Türkei ausgewandert.

Meine Großeltern sprechen immer noch kein gutes deutsch

Wir sprechen oft türkisch zu Hause

* … zu Bairan essen wir türkisch
* Mein Vater und ich gehen in die Moschee
* Das ist ein großes Essen mit vielen türkischen Spezialitäten

* Hast du immer noch Verwandten in der Türkei? – Ich habe jede Menge Tanten, etc.

* Wir sehen uns alle zwei Jahre, wenn wir auf Urlaub sind.

Deutsch
* Eigentlich bin ich hier geboren.

* In Dortmund
* Meine Mutter ist Deutsche

* Deine Muttersprache? – Eigentlich deutsch.
* Zwei- bis dreimal pro Woche gehen wir aus – zum Fußballtraining, in den Jugendklub oder ins Kino.

* Wir gehen besonders gern zu McDonalds, wo mein Lieblingsessen ein Big Mac ist.
* Ich habe allerlei Freunde.

* Am liebsten fahre ich im Winter nach Österreich zum Skifahren

Quick Test (p. 91)

Perfect Tense:

1 *Wir haben eine Hafenrundfahrt gemacht.*
2 *… haben wir in einer kleinen Pension gewohnt.*
3 *… haben wir den Fernsehturm besichtigt.*
4 *… bin ich mit meiner Familie nach Hamburg gefahren.*

Quick Test (p. 91)

Imperfect Tense:

1 *Sonntagvormittags gingen wir zum Fischmarkt.*
2 *… weil sie da auf der Universität arbeiteten.*
3 *Aber noch besser waren die fantastischen Torten.*
4 *Für €15 konnte man mit dem Aufzug nach oben fahren.*
5 *Das waren alte Warenhäuser.*
6 *Zu der Zeit wohnten Freunde…*

Grammar

Cases and articles
Quick Test (p. 93)
1 *Seine*
2 *Dem Mann*
3 *Einer*

Prepositions and pronouns
Quick Test (p. 95)
Prepositions

1 *der, die*
2 *der, dem*
3 *einen*
4 *das*
5 *den*
6 *den*
7 *der*
8 *einem*
9 *den, die*
10 *einem*

Quick Test (p. 96)
Pronouns

1 *ihr*
2 *ihn*
3 *mich*
4 *ihnen*
5 *ihn*
6 *dir*

Verbs – present & perfect tense
Grammar Test 1 (p. 98)
The Present Tense

1 *essen* = to eat, *haben* = to have, *lesen* = to read, *nehmen* = to take, *treffen* =to meet
2 *essen – du isst, er / sie / es / man isst*
haben – du hast, er / sie / es / man hat
lesen – du liest, er / sie / es / man liest
nehmen – du nimmst, er / sie / es / man nimmt
treffen – du triffst, er / sie / es / man trifft
3 To be checked by your teacher.

Quick Test (p. 99)
The Past Tense

1 *Hast, gesehen*
2 *habe, gekauft*
3 *sind, gegangen*
4 *hat, gefüttert*
5 *Bist, gekommen*
6 *haben, gegessen*
7 *bist, geblieben*
8 *hat, geregnet*
9 *bin, geflogen*
10 *Haben, geschrieben*

Imperfect & future tenses
Quick Test (p. 101)
The Imperfect Tense

1 When were you in (the) town?
2 There was nothing to do there!
3 When I was young I had a dog.
4 My mother picked me up from the station.
5 My father used to like cooking.
6 We went to a party.

Quick Test (p. 102)
The Future Tense

1 *werden*
2 *wirst*
3 *werde*
4 *wird*

Translations

1 Next year we will fly / go / travel to America.
2 What will you do?
3 I will get a good report.
4 In ten years' time he will be bald.

Separable verbs, reflexive verbs & adjectives
Separable verbs
Quick Test (p. 103)
Present Tense:

1 *Ich **stehe** morgens um 7 Uhr **auf**. (aufstehen)*
2 *Herr Maier **kommt** heute nachmittag **zurück**. (zurückkommen)*
3 ***Machen** Sie bitte die Tür **zu**! (zumachen)*

Perfect Tense:

4 *Die Gäste haben Geschenke **mitgebracht**. (mitbringen)*
5 *Der Bus ist an mir **vorbeigefahren**. (vorbeifahren)*
6 *Die Passagiere sind am Marktplatz **ausgestiegen**. (aussteigen)*

Reflexive verbs
Quick Test (p. 104)
1 *Ich putze mir die Zähne. / Ich habe mir die Zähne geputzt.*
2 *Ich ziehe mich an. / Ich habe mich angezogen.*
3 *Ich kämme mich. / Ich habe mich gekämmt.*
4 *Ich schminke mich. / Ich habe mich geschminkt.*
5 *Ich beeile mich. / Ich habe mich beeilt.*
6 *Ich treffe mich (mit meinen Freunden) / Ich habe mich (mit meinen Freunden) getroffen.*

Adjectives
Quick Test (p. 106)
1d: 2f: 3a: 4c: 5b: 6e

Inversion & subordinate clauses
Inversion
Quick Test (p. 108)
1 *Oft gehe ich einkaufen.*
2 *Ab und zu spielt er Tennis.*
3 *Jeden Freitag gehen meine Freunde schwimmen.*
4 *Zweimal pro Woche arbeitet sie im Sportgeschäft.*
5 *Jeden Abend muss ich Vokabeln lernen.*
6 *Letzte Woche habe ich mir eine neue Hose gekauft.*

Subordinate clauses
Quick Test (p. 110)
1 *Da ich kein Geld habe, gehe ich nicht aus.*
2 *Ich lerne gern Deutsch, weil die Grammatik so einfach ist.*
3 *Wenn das Wetter gut ist, spielen wir gern Fußball.*
4 *Ich war noch hungrig, obwohl ich schon gefrühstückt hatte.*
Make up four other sentences like the ones above. Remember to ask your teacher to check them.

Some basic language

Time – Manner – Place
Quick Test (p. 111)

1 *Gestern sind wir langsam nach Hause gekommen.*
2 *Ich gehe oft mit meinen Freunden ins Kino.*
3 *Jeden Morgen ist der Lehrer schlechter Laune in der Mathestunde.*
4 *Nachmittags kommen die Kinder glücklich nach Hause.*
5 *Um elf Uhr ist Anja müde ins Bett gegangen.*
6 *Als ich jung war, ging ich gern zu meiner Oma.*

Um ... zu ...
Quick Test (p. 112)

1 *Klaus macht immer seine Hausaufgaben, um gute Noten zu bekommen.*
2 *Ich habe einen Nebenjob, um Geld zu verdienen.*
3 *Viele Leute kommen in die Stadt, um Arbeitsplätze zu suchen.*
4 *Opa trägt eine Brille, um besser zu sehen.*
5 *Ich esse viel Obst und Gemüse, um gesund zu bleiben.*
6 *Vater und Mutter gehen ins Theater, um ein neues Theaterstück zu sehen.*

Time
Quick Test (p. 114)

1 *Halb zehn.*
2 *Zehn nach sechs.*
3 *Halb neun.*
4 *Zwanzig vor zwölf.*
5 *Viertel vor elf.*
6 *Fünfundzwanzig nach zehn.*
7 *Viertel nach drei.*
8 *Halb eins.*

1 Quarter past seven.
2 Half past two.
3 Quarter to four.
4 Twenty-five past past eleven.
5 Half past twelve.
6 Quarter past twelve.
7 Ten to six.
8 Half past ten.

Model folios 1

Quick Test (p. 116)

Subordinate clauses:

1 *Wir fliegen immer, weil es praktisch und billig ist, ...*
2 *und weil man schnell dahin kommt.*
3 *wenn das Wetter sehr heiß ist und viele Touristen unterwegs sind.*
4 *weil sie fast alles bezahlen.*
5 *wenn sie so viele Sehenswürdigkeiten besichtigen.*
6 *als ich dreizehn war.*
7 *als der Urlaub vorbei war.*

Conditional:

1 *Mein Traumurlaub wäre in Australien.*
2 *Ich würde gern eine Tour durch den Kontinent machen,*
3 *ich möchte so viele Länder wie möglich sehen.*

Example of a **starter** sentence:
Meiner Meinung nach *sind die Spanier sehr freundlich.*

Example of **Subordinate** word order:
Ich wohne gern in Schottland, weil es schön ist.

Example of the **Imperfect**:
Sie kamen regelmäßig nach Schottland.

Example of **Conditional**:
Wenn ich viel Geld **hätte**, **würde** *ich teuere Kleidung kaufen.*

Model folios 2

How good is this essay?
Quick Test (p. 118)

Time phrases:

Im Juli	In July
Wenn das Wetter schön / schlecht ist	When the weather is good / bad
tagsüber	during the day
den ganzen Tag / Abend	the whole day / evening
Dieses Jahr	This year
am Abend	in the evening
Letztes Jahr	Last year
vor drei Jahren	three years ago
als ich ... war	when I was

Adjectival phrases:

den ganzen Tag / Abend	The whole evening/night
Auf der anderen Seite	On the other hand
für kleine Kinder	For small children
eine gute Atmosphäre	A good atmosphere
ein fantastisches T-Shirt	A fantastic T-Shirt
mein bester Geburtstag	My best birthday
eiskalte Getränke	Ice-cold drinks
in ein kleines Restaurant	In (into) a small restaurant
fantastische Pizza	Fantastic pizza
auf nächsten Juli	To next July

Index